Working With The Mineral Kingdom

A Gemstone Recipe Book

By Karen E. Wood

Copyright © 2017 Karen E. Wood
All rights reserved.
ISBN: 6926258
ISBN-13: 978-1543051445
Revision 2

DEDICATION

In Memory of Barbara Wood
Thank you to all who have supported me on my life path, especially KMP and CA

Acknowledgements/References

"The Crystal Bible: A Definitive Guide To Crystals" by Judy Hall, Published by Godsfield, Press, Lgd. Laurel House, Station Approach, Aresford, Hampshire 5024 9JH, UK, Distributed by Walking Stick Press, Ohio

"Love Is In The Earth: A Kaleidoscope of Crystals" by Melody. Updated. Published by Earth-Love Publishing House, 3440 Youngfield Street, Suite 353, Wheat Ridge, Colorado 80033 USA.

"The Book of Stones: Who They Are and What They Teach?" by Robert Simmons and Naisha Ahsian with contributions by Hazel Raven. Published by Heaven and Earth Publishing, LLC, PO Box 249, East Montpelier, VT 05651.

.

Caution: The information in this book is not intended to act as a substitute for medical treatment, nor can it be used for diagnosis. Crystals/gemstones are from the mineral kingdom and should not be abused or misused. Seek professional advice if you have health care issues or any doubts about a mineral's components. The recipes and information in this book is to impart information and does not guarantee a cure or that the formula will work for you. Each body's chemistry is different, and certain minerals work better for some people and not others. Always seek medical advice for serious conditions

CONTENTS

	Introduction	Pg 3
1	**Understanding, Cleansing and Working with Gemstones**	Pg 7
2	**Gridding**	Pg 15
3	**Mandalas, Altars and Medicine Wheels**	Pg 21
4	**Making Elixirs**	Pg 25
5	**Emotional Behaviors, Addictions and Bad Habits**	Pg 35
6	**Immune Building, Colds/Flu/Respiratory**	Pg 43
7	**Pain, Joints and Bones**	Pg 49
8	**Heart Disease & Chronic Conditions**	Pg 55
9	**Eyes, Ears, Skin**	Pg 69
10	**Miscellaneous Recipes**	Pg 73
11	**Index**	Pg 91

Enjoy working with the mineral kingdom.
Blessings to all.

INTRODUCTION

"You will find something more in woods than in books. Trees and stones will teach you that which you can never learn from masters." - Saint Bernard

If you are like me, you have had a fascination with gemstones, crystals and the Earth for years, but didn't understand the connection. I would go into a store and just stare or admire the geodes, clusters and specimens, always wanting to buy them and bring them home, but not knowing why. As time went by, the attraction to gemstones and minerals became so strong that I began my collection without really knowing much about them or really understanding their properties.

Now, some people simply collect them for their coloring, their natural looks, their chemical properties or their monetary value, but I collected them because they made me feel good. Little did I know at that time about their metaphysical properties. I was soon to learn; however, that these little pieces of Earth had their own energy and ideas about what our relationship was going to be.

I was a lot older when I started exploring the metaphysical end of the mineral kingdom. As a child, and even a young adult, I would often find myself looking at specimens of rocks, not jewelry or fine cut gemstones, but the raw, unpolished version. I would walk away wondering, "What would I do with the stone?" and "Why did I want it in the first place?"

I did some research, collected some gemstones from a metaphysical store and started experimenting for myself to see if what I was reading was true. The first book I read was "The Crystal Bible" by Judy Hall. I would highly recommend this book, as well as her "Crystal Bible 2" for the beginning collector. A few other books, such as "The Book of Stones" by Naisha Ashian and Robert Simmons; and "Love is in the Earth – A Kaleidoscope of Crystals" by Melody, are very informative and excellent reference books, describing the physical composition, as well as the metaphysical properties of individual gemstones. Not long after starting my collection, I found that the gemstones worked for me, but still wondered if it was because of my preconceived notions and the different things I have read.

When a co-worker at the private preschool daycare where I was working asked me if there was something I could do for her older dog that was going deaf and blind, I made an elixir with a combination of gemstones to see if it would help. About a week after she had started putting the elixir in the dog's water, she told me she saw an improvement in the dog. The dog showed signs of being able to hear a car pull up in the driveway and would meet its owner at the door - something it hadn't done in a long time. Within a few weeks, the dog was able to see treats being handed to it instead of having to sniff out where they were. This positive result made a believer out of me because the dog didn't know there was anything different in its water, but the impact these elements had showed a clear correlation.

A lot of children have an interest in stones and may come home with pockets full when out playing. After starting my collection, I would have a few stones in my pocket while working at the daycare. One day, the children were not listening to the teachers, arguing amongst themselves and not playing nicely. I took out my Chalcedony and held it in my palm. I talked to the rock in front of the children, telling the stone that it wasn't doing its job properly. A couple of the children saw and heard me, stopped their arguing and came over to see what I had in my hand. The other children then noticed and also came over. They asked me what the stone was supposed to do, and I told them it was supposed to make everyone get along nicely - in harmony. The children showed a great interest in the stone and asked what others I had.

Every day after that I would show them what "rocks" I had in my pocket and tell them each one's name, as well as describe what it's 'job' was. They learned quickly and loved finding out more about the stones. Many of the children remembered the stones names and their duties, then started their own collections. One day I brought an agate to the school and as usual, one student who was most interested in the stones asked me what it did. I said, "Why don't you tell me what is does?" and sure enough, he did! This student intuitively picked up on the energy of the stone and was able to tell me a few of its metaphysical properties. These young souls are much more in tune with the Earth, with the metaphysical and the "magic" of the universe; however, everyone has intuitive abilities. It is up to you whether you want to develop them.

Gemstones are a nice tool for helping fine-tune your intuitive abilities, as well as opening yourself up spiritually and emotionally. Déjà vu, knowing who is calling on the phone as it rings and thinking of someone then hearing from them, is proof that we are more intuitive than we realize. One of the funniest ways I started to trust my inner voice or intuition was when I stopped at a fast food restaurant on my way home from work. I ordered food for my friend and a sandwich for myself, then waited in line for the drive up window. Sitting there I heard in my head "Check the order; there is a sandwich missing." I brushed it off two more times, paid and drove home never checking the bag. When I got home I handed my friend the bag and went to change out of my work clothes. I heard my friend call from the kitchen, "Didn't you get yourself anything?" My sandwich was, in fact, missing – another lesson learned!
.
***"All the stones that are around here, each one has a language of its own. Even the earth has a song."
– Wallace Black Elk, LAKOTA***

The Native American people believe that all things have a soul or energy. Though they seem to be dead or unfeeling, gemstones and crystals have energy and vibrations. Where do our bodies come from, what are we all made up of? Mother Earth. There is an old saying, ashes to ashes, dust to dust. If we are living, breathing energy forms made from the earth, it is only natural to believe we are interconnected to animals, plants and stones. Science tells us our bodies need vitamins and minerals to live a healthy life. The mineral kingdom gives us what our bodies need by vibration, as well as nutritional absorption. The gemstone Shungite comes from Russia, has been studied there for many years and is documented to slow down cancer growth, battle infections, remove bacteria, toxins and heavy metals from the body as well as shield the body from harmful electro-magnetic radiation from Wi-Fi, microwaves, computers, cellphones and more.

There are many good books on crystals and gemstones that focus on the individual or family of stones and the function of each individually. However, very few books are dedicated to different combinations of gemstones to use for elixirs or energy work. (An elixir is mineral water made up of the vibration of the gemstones you put into the water.) Some books contain a few grid layouts, what a single stone can do metaphysically, emotionally and physically. There are many questions still left unanswered - such as which stones to use for treating specific conditions, how to make an elixir or tincture, how to create a mandala, altar or medicine wheel of gemstones. Spirit/The Creator has inspired me to put together a recipe book of elixirs, which is less traditional than the books already on the market.

The most important thing to remember whenever you use a gemstone (for meditation, energy work, raising your vibration, emotional stability, etc.) is your intention. Always set your intention for the highest good. Focus on what you want to accomplish and then manifest it. Make sure to use gemstones that you are drawn to or resonate with. Don't just go with what it says in a book or what someone else tells you. You are unique, and so are your vibrations. What gemstone or crystal works for one person in a specific way may not be as powerful for another person. Just like we have different energy fields, blood types, personalities and chemical make-ups, we still have a lot in common, and like reading a general horoscope that will be true for a lot of people, it will be way off the mark for others. It is always best to see what stones you are attracted to and what would work best for your uniqueness. Substitute any stone that doesn't feel right. Using raw, tumbled or lower-grade gemstones does not affect the vibration it emits, so don't worry if you can't find the perfectly faceted stone. If you don't have a specific stone, use clear quartz and program it to be any stone you need. Don't be fooled by "experts," who try to sell you high-priced gemstones, gimmicks or mineral water.

One of the most difficult questions I am often asked is, "What does this gemstone do?" Every gemstone has so many different characteristics – physically, emotionally, intellectually, energetically and spiritually. It would take a very long time to describe all the benefits of each stone. Trust your instinct – there is a reason why you are picking a particular stone. When you research its properties, there is usually an "ah ha" moment when you see what applies to you.

Many of today's prescription medicines are made of crystals or metals like lithium.

The plant, animal and human kingdoms all depend upon the mineral kingdom to live. The mineral kingdom is rich in nutrients that reach plants through water and soil. The animal and human kingdoms absorb the minerals and nutrients when eating the plants or drinking water. Minerals are trace amounts of the earth that are absorbed by plants, animals and humans. Our bodies need vitamins and minerals on a daily basis in order to function properly.

Some well-known minerals are calcium (Calcite), copper, iron, magnesium (magnesite), phosphorus (Apatite), selenium (Selenite) and zinc (Zincite). Many important chemicals are created from Calcite, as well as useful drugs. Petalite (lithium aluminum silicate) was discovered in a Swedish iron mine, and lithium salts were used in the 19th Century to treat gout. Lithium is used to treat bipolar disorder and depression, as well as a preventive treatment for migraine headaches. Gemstones can aid us in our quest for health, but seek experienced medical advice when necessary.

Minerals also contain the most important ingredient to all the kingdoms – energy.

Just as we have different organs in our body to perform separate functions, the Earth contains various minerals that have different functions to perform. Minerals vibrate with energetic frequencies, and each has a specific frequency of vibration. Depending on the vibration, we can initiate an emotional or physical healing, spiritual attunement or awakening and a higher state of consciousness when using gemstones.

The slower frequencies or vibrations combine into larger particles and become matter - like the hard stones or our physical bodies. Our thoughts and spiritual selves vibrate higher than can be measured by today's methods, but these "light" or "spirit" vibrations can be perceptible through our intuition. Cravings for certain foods may indicate our need for certain vitamins or minerals. We are drawn to specific gemstones at certain times because our body needs that vibration or energy to treat a lack or condition we may have.

Want to understand more of how they work? Try this experiment. Put a clear quartz crystal in one glass of water, a rose quartz in another glass of water and an amethyst in a third glass of water. Leave in the refrigerator overnight. In the morning, take a sip of each one and taste the difference. They are all from the quartz family, yet each one of them works in a different way and so tastes different as well. I use a clear quartz tumbled stone to purify my drinking water. I boil water in my stainless steel teakettle, and once the water has cooled, I pour it into a glass pitcher (that has a lid) and add the clear quartz stone. When the water has been left for a few hours, it tastes like spring water and has a sweeter or purer taste. A gentleman and his wife were selling a water purification system at my friend's herb store and didn't believe me when I told him what I did to purify my water. The man said, 'It may purify, but what about the alkalinity?" He asked if he could test my water, and I told him to go ahead. When he saw that my water was better than that which came out of his filter, he was shocked. In fact, he, his wife and one assistant bought a bunch of tumbled clear quartz crystals before they left.

You can make mineral water or gemstone elixirs and add them to a favorite beverage, in cooking, baking or make your herbal teas with them. Gemstones are tools that can aid us in our work of harmonizing our energetic, physical and spiritual bodies in order to empower ourselves. In this way, they can help us to heal our bodies, emotions and spirit or to aid us in identifying our life or soul's purpose, as well as strengthen our divine connections. Gemstones will work with you and help support you in your lifestyle changes.

The suggested recipes I have included in this book have been intuitively combined and are based on the more easily obtainable and less-expensive stones. They are a guidepost to follow, based on what has worked for me, people I know and what I believe will work for most people and animals. Feel free to use only a couple of stones in each category or add those you feel are necessary. There is no expert or higher authority - use your own intuition. Your body and spirit are unique and your elixirs will reflect that. These recipes are to get you started and to inspire/motivate you. They are examples of physical, emotional, energetic, intellectual and spiritual balancing stones for each condition or issue to be treated. Reflect upon your issue or disease and pick the stone(s) that are best for you. Not all stones or illnesses are presented in this book.

I suggest putting together a gemstone first-aid kit. The minimum amount of stones in this kit would be: Amethyst, Carnelian, Clear Quartz, Rose Quartz and Shungite. I also recommend expanding this kit to include: Amber, Black Tourmaline, Bloodstone, Citrine, Blue Lace Agate, Iolite, Red Jasper and Selenite. These additional stones will allow you to balance your chakras as well as provide protection from negativity.

***Definition of Disease** - a disorder of structure or function in a human, animal or plant, especially one that produces specific signs or symptoms or that affects a specific location and is not simply a direct result of physical injury.*

***Definition of Dis-ease** - Dis-ease is a hyphenated variation of the word "disease." The term dis-ease is used by individuals and healing communities who are aligned with wellness, choosing not to empower health issues by focusing on a particular ailment. The intent is to place emphasis on the natural state of "ease" being imbalanced or disrupted.*

***Definition of Healing** – Harmony of the physical, emotional, energetic, intellectual and spiritual bodies. The mineral kingdom helps to bring harmony to all the bodies. Minerals are an important tool for the body's immune system, as are vitamins.*

CHAPTER ONE – Understanding, Cleansing and Working with Gemstones

"Crystals are a living energy... Mother Earth's gifts to us, formed within Her body. In a mystical and beauty-full way, they are the keys to the Universe." — Angie Karan

When selecting your crystals or gemstones, go with your gut, and choose those to which you are being drawn. What feels right is more important than how it looks. Think of how you will use the stone. A large, rough, raw piece is good for the environment in altars, mandalas or just placed in a room, but a small tumbled stone would work better for your pockets, jewelry, elixirs and under your pillow. Everyone is intuitive, you just have to work at it and allow yourself to progress.

Many years ago, I was attracted to a Strawberry Quartz bracelet, but I am not a big fan of pink. Every time I went into the store, I was being drawn to the bracelet. I had researched the properties of Strawberry Quartz, but nothing stood out as to why I needed it. Finally, I bought the bracelet and started wearing it. After three days, I noticed my allergy to proteins in dairy foods wasn't as bad. Drinking my daily iced coffee with extra cream and sugar, I wasn't getting the mucus buildup like I usually did. The research I did had nothing listed about Strawberry Quartz reducing or eliminating mucus, but that is what it did for me.

People often ask me which stone to use for a certain condition, and intuitively, I tune into their energy fields and chemical make up. I will often intuit a stone that is not known for that condition, or I have them hold different stones that are known for that condition, one at a time, for a few minutes, to let them feel how their bodies' individual chemistry interact with the stone(s). For instance, if the stone feels hot or cold, if the pain or discomfort they are feeling decreases or increases, if their mood changes for better or worse or if they feel nauseous, uncomfortable or get a headache.

Some people say they don't feel anything when holding stones, but still want to work with gemstones. Everyone is intuitive, you just have to work at it like anything else. Just because you don't feel anything doesn't mean you are not intuitive. You can be drawn to a stone by its looks and when you look up its characteristics, you will have an "ah-ha" moment because it will work on something you are experiences spiritually, emotionally, physically, intellectually or energetically. The more you pay attention to your how your body or mind reacts to a stone, the quicker you will grow intuitively.

I had just started collecting stones and bought the book, "The Crystal Bible" by Judy Hall. I was reading it cover to cover and exploring the stones alphabetically. I was on the "Bs" when I was riding to work one day and the word "Chalcedony" popped into my head. It was like reading a road sign. I had no idea what the word meant, where it came from, nor that it was actually a type of stone. A few days later I was into the "Cs" and came across the stone's description. Reading the properties was an eye opener for me. I went to my first gemstone show about two weeks later and saw one vendor setting up her booth. I didn't want to interrupt her, so started to browse the gemstones she had already placed on the table. There were many stones on the table, but I immediately saw a beautiful black-and-white stone with swirls and spirals amongst a few others of the same kind. It really caught my eye, and I was drawn to it. I had no idea what the stone was. The vendor took a break from setting up her booth and I asked her if she had any Chalcedony. She said she did, but didn't think she had unpacked them yet. I asked her about the black-and-white stones on the other side of the table and when she looked over at them, she replied "Oh, there they are." Even though I had never seen the stone and the ones on the table didn't resemble the picture in the book, I instinctively picked it out amongst the large selection of stones in the booth.

Once you are drawn to a stone, hold it for a few minutes and see how it affects you. If you get a dizzy, uncomfortable or nauseous feeling, put it down immediately. If it feels warm, inviting or tingling, then it is a stone for you. The stone that makes you uncomfortable is not a stone you need at this time as it may be too powerful. If you feel you can't leave the stone behind, you probably will need it in the future, so go ahead and acquire it. Just don't work with it until you are ready. Investigate the metaphysical, physical, spiritual and emotional elements of the stone and find another stone that has similar properties and doesn't make you react in a negative way. Work with this stone until you feel ready to move forward. This may take only a few minutes or after many sessions. Never work with a stone for more than 20 minutes at a time and not more than twice a day, as you can throw off your physical body or unbalance your energetic bodies.

I met a man who loves Moldavite and was working with it constantly. A few weeks after I met him, he came into the store where I teach and said he had been in hospital earlier in the week for extremely high blood pressure and heart issues. The doctors did all kinds of test, used different drugs and techniques to bring down his blood pressure and kept him overnight until his blood pressure was finally under control. He never had a history of high blood pressure or heart disease. When he was ultimately released from the hospital, his case was marked as an anomaly because they didn't know what caused it. After talking with him about our mutual love of gemstones, he told me he loved Moldavite and has a large collection of them. He told me that the day before he went into the hospital he was feeling wonderful and worked with 7 Moldavites placed at different points on his body while laying down. This man had not worked with stones very much, but had been collecting them over a long period of time because he liked the look of the stones. He had just started getting into the metaphysical end of things and didn't do any research or heard the warnings that they could have an adverse effect. He was very surprised when I told him that he might have ended up in the hospital because of the Moldavite throwing everything out of whack. The high vibration of Moldavite changed his body's vibrations. Working with so many pieces of Moldavite and for a long period of time was the equivalent of drinking a six pack of an energy drink that has large quantities of caffeine. It is okay to work with higher vibration stones, but you must remember to ground yourself and not work with them for too long. It is the intention you set that empowers them and this man wanted to feel the "high" or disconnection that Moldavite gives him.

If you acquire a stone in a ring, pendant, bracelet or other piece of jewelry, be aware of how it makes you feel while wearing it for a long period of time. If you feel tired, drained or a headache coming on, take off your jewelry and see how you feel without it. Sometimes the vibration in the jewelry is interfering with our energy and telling us we don't need to be working with it at this time. Our mood will often define which jewelry or clothing we choose to wear on any given day and once our vibration has changed or mood uplifted, our needs have been met. Don't forget to clean your jewelry or recharge it after wearing it for long periods of time.

After you have chosen your new friend(s) and have brought it/them home, it is time for cleaning. Even though it may look clean to the eye, you do not know what trauma your friend has been through since being unearthed. (Even if you do not believe in a living energy in the stone, it is still a good idea to clean it because of all the people who may have handled it before you.)

Depending upon what kind of stone you have, as well as your own personal style and preference, there are many ways to clean it. Smudging, running water, dry sea salt, water/sea salt solution, sound, breath or energy (reiki) are the most popular ways of cleaning. I will address each one briefly.

When in doubt, check the chemical compound of the stone or just use a "safe" method, i.e., smudging, energy cleansing, or stone cleaning. Some stones will dissolve in water, get scratched or dulled by salt or are too brittle to handle. This same principle should be used when making an elixir.

Smudging. This is a way of cleaning your stone without harming it - especially if you have a very fragile stone, such as a cluster. This technique is preferred by collectors and healers who wish to purify the stone with the four elements by using an abalone shell, sage, a feather and matches.

Running water. If you are fortunate enough to live near the ocean, a natural spring or river, you can cleanse the stones by putting them into a netted bag or nylon hosiery that will allow the running water to cleanse them without washing the stones away. Natural spring water should be used whenever possible. You can use tap water but with all the chemical and mineral contents in today's water, it is not the suggested method. Some stones that should not be exposed to water cleansing are Azurite, Calcite, Halite, Pyrite, Selenite, Kyanite, Sulfur and fragile clusters because of their water solubility and frailty.

Dry sea salt. You can employ the dry sea salt method for most stones. Get a shallow container, pour a generous amount of sea salt into it, and then place the stones gently into the salt. Next, pour more salt over the stones until they are completely covered, and then let them sit overnight. The next morning, simply brush or blow off the salt, and they'll shine beautifully. Stones that will scratch easily or may lose their water content such as Malachite, Moldavite and Opal should not be cleansed by the dry-salt method. When opal is left in dry salt for too long it can actually change into chalcedony.

Water/sea salt solution. This method combines spring water with sea salt (the average solution is 2 tablespoons salt to 1 pint water). Soak the stones for one to 24 hours, then remove, and rinse with clean spring water. Just remember that not all stones like water or salt. Or if you live near the ocean, you can put your friends in mesh bag and gently cleanse them in the sea by holding the bag securely while the waves wash over it.

Sound. Using tuning forks, singing bowls, drumming and bells are ways to evoke vibrational cleaning. The stones react to the pitch or vibration and release any negative energy it may have stored. "Love Is In The Earth: A Kaleidoscope of Crystals" by Melody features the vibrational tone of each stone, as well as its numeric element.

Breath/energy. If you do not have any way of using any of the above methods and want to cleanse your stone immediately, you may employ either the breath or energy cleaning method. Clear your mind, hold the stone lightly in your fingers and blow gently on it, thinking of removing any negative energy and sending it into the Earth where it will be changed into positive energy. Similarly, when doing energy cleansing, clear your mind, place the stone in your palm and envision a light field surrounding the stone and removing any dark or negative energy. *[This method is also how to program and charge your crystal for personal use. Hold the crystal loosely in your upraised palm, and imagine a white light shining upon it, cleansing and charging it. In your mind, have a conversation with the stone about what you'd like the stone to do for you. Accept its gentle vibration and thank it for its healing energy.]*

Stones to clean stones. Use a Clear Quartz cluster or a Carnelian to cleanse your other gemstones. Position the gemstones to be cleaned on or next to a Clear Quartz cluster or place a Carnelian amongst a small selection of stones and leave overnight. When using the Clear Quartz cluster for cleansing, you also are recharging the stones and just have to set your intention when you work with your stones again.

Bury in the earth. Our stones are such faithful healers and workers; they need a little vacation in order to recharge. You can bury them in the earth (mark the spot so you can find them again!) or get a terracotta or clay plant pot to bury them in. Leave them for a couple of weeks or as long as six months, depending upon their depleted energy. You can also "gift" the Earth and the elements with your stone by burying it in the forest or putting it into the ocean or a river.

Now that your gemstone or mineral collection has been cleansed and energized, it is time to work with them. Relax and try sitting quietly for 5-10 minutes with a crystal in your palm. Shut your eyes, and just let your mind contemplate the crystal/gemstone you are holding. You will be surprised at the thoughts and feelings you experience during that time. If you experience pain, nausea, a headache or feel too much pressure in your head, stop this meditation immediately. If you experience these symptoms when wearing gemstone jewelry, take each piece off and see if the symptoms disappear. These crystals may be too powerful for you at this time. Try working with less intense crystals.

There are many ways to use your mineral kingdom friends – wearing them as jewelry, keeping stones in your pocket, under your pillow, gridding, in a mandala or healing layout, on an altar or as an elixir. Make a mineral elixir and add it to drinking water or to an herbal tea, use it in cooking, baking and water for plants and pets.

I have a magnetic hematite bracelet that I have used as a headband, anklet and necklace. I have many gemstone bracelets that I wear, as well as using them for mineral water. Have a tall, thin drinking glass? Put a gemstone bracelet around it and fill it with your favorite beverage. If you leave it on the glass long enough, the mineral vibrations will enter your water as well as the drinking glass. This is a great indirect way of making mineral water. Place the water in the glass, slide on the bracelet and put it into the refrigerator for a few hours. Add a few bracelets if you want a combination of minerals.

I use my bracelets to add gemstones to my prayers. I have a tall, white candle in a thin glass cylinder. I slide different bracelets onto the glass cylinder to add the gemstone's metaphysical and healing properties to my prayers. I also do this when I make a mandala or altar with a candle as my centerpiece.

You can also place gemstones around your plants, under your pet's water dish (make sure it is large enough so the pet will not swallow or choke if it comes out from under the bowl), even as a zipper pull. Let your creativity and imagination be your guide - just make sure you use gemstones safely. Never place them within reach of small children as they can appear pretty and candy-like. Below are some of the basic ways to use gemstones.

Pockets, Amulet Bags, Bras – Indirect healing; slower, gentler, general application.
Mandalas/Feng Shui – Environmental - stress, disease, surrounding energy for elixir, protection
Jewelry – Direct method of healing, precision placement, heart, wrist/pulse point, fingers, etc.
Chakras – Energy balancing, harmony of bodies
Gridding – Placing gemstones around your home, office, plants or person
Altars – Spiritual use for prayer or personal growth
Holding in palms – Meditation and focused intention upon area needing healing
Elixir – Making mineral water for consumption; infusing the water with gemstone vibrations
Shapes and colors

Gemstones points and spheres have been used for centuries in diagnosing illnesses and problems, healing, self-empowerment, foretelling the future and soul travel. The most common use of the sphere however, is self improvement or for getting in touch with your intuitive side. It has been used in scrying and divination for problem-solving throughout history by different cultures.

Sphere gazing allows you to open your mind, heart, and clarify your thoughts, emotions, and discern the paths you should take. It aids us in getting in touch with our deepest thoughts, desires, dreams, and Higher/Self or Spirit. Gazing into the sphere, we perceive symbols, colors, shapes, windows, tunnels and receive impressions which help us understand our own experiences. It is just like seeing shapes in clouds, inkblot testing by psychologists, dream interpretation, reading tea leaves or inspirational divination cards. These are tools to help us heal, grow in knowledge and wisdom, and assist in getting to know ourselves.

For healing purposes, a sphere or rounded edge has a softer, balanced energy flow versus a point which is a focused beam like a laser. If you are working on a small area and want a more intense vibration, then you would use a gemstone point. If you want to work on a larger area, then you would use a spherical shape. Think of a lamp versus a spotlight.

A single pointed crystal or wand works like a laser beam on a small point. When you face the point toward you, it brings you energy. Facing the point away from you draws off negative energy or creates a protective grid.

A double-terminated crystal has a point on both ends which allows a stronger energy to flow in both directions. An energy worker may use this type of crystal to strengthen the healing bond between the client and self. This crystal also can be used to channel angelic or The Great Spirit's energy as well as energy from our earth mother.

A pyramid will pull from all four directions and focus, as well as amplify your intention into a beam of energy pointing upward and carry your message, feelings or intention to the Divine.

A generator will work in a similar way to the pyramid, but it has more planes or faces near the top point causing the energy to spread out – more like many rays of sunshine instead of a single beam.

A crystal bowl will work like a sphere spreading its energy and sound vibrations in soft waves.

Using specific colored gemstones that correspond to the colors of the chakras is a basic understanding of which gemstones to use for certain treatments. (It is a good idea to balance your chakras at least once a month, but don't do it more than once a week unless you have been ill or have gone through an emotional or traumatic episode. If putting the stones directly on your chakras, don't leave the stones on for more than 20 minutes at a time.) The colors of gemstones don't always have to match the chakra color and can work on more than just one chakra. Clear Quartz can work on any chakra, any part of the physical or energetic body as well as for emotional issues. You can also use chakra wands or jewelry. Just be sure to cleanse and recharge before wearing or using again. Also keep brightly colored gemstones out of the direct sun as it will cause them to fade.

These are a few common stones to be cautious with when cleaning or placement in the home. Many stones can fade in direct sunlight. Remember their homes are in the earth and it is unnatural for them to be in the sun for long periods.

For a comprehensive listing of cleaning methods as well as which ones to keep out of direct sunlight when gridding, I recommend "The Crystal Bible" (1 & 2) by Judy Hall or "Love Is In The Earth: A Kaleidoscope of Crystals" by Melody. These are also good reference books for those stones that cannot be used directly in water or that may be toxic in an elixir. Do not use any stones that have a metallic or

Sulfur component by the direct method. When in doubt, use the indirect method.

No Salt Cleaning
Aventurine
Azeztulite
Azurite
Chalcedony with Water Inclusion
Clusters
Fluorite
Labradorite
Malachite
Moldavite,
Okenite
Onyx
Opal

Use Indirect/ No Water/Salt Water Cleaning/
Acanthite (breaks down in water/too soft)
Actinolite (asbestos)
Amber (pine resin – safe but breaks down in water)
Alexandrite (copper)
Atacamite (copper)
Aquamarine (aluminum)
Azurite (arsenic)
Bixbite (aluminum)
Black Tourmaline (aluminum)
Calcite (breaks down in water)
Cavansite (aluminum)
Chalcopyrite (copper)
Chrysocolla (copper)
Cinnabar (mercury based/toxic)
Clusters (brittle or raw stones)
Copper (toxic in large doses)
Cuprite (copper)
Dioptase (copper)
Dumortierite (aluminum)
Emerald (aluminum)
Fluorite (toxic)
Galena (lead based)
Garnet (aluminum)
Halite (salt – breaks down in water)
Hiddenite (aluminum)

Iolite (aluminum)
Kunzite (aluminum)
Labradorite (aluminum)
Lapis Lazuli (Sulfur/pyrite)
Lepidolite (aluminum)
Malachite (Sulfur)
Moldavite (aluminum oxide)
Moonstone (aluminum)
Morganite (aluminum)
Okenite (fibrous- breaks easily)
Prehnite (aluminum)
Pyrite (Sulfur)
Ruby (aluminum)
Sapphire (aluminum)
Selenite (breaks down in water)
Sodalite (aluminum)
Spinel (aluminum)
Staurolite (aluminum)
Stibnite (lead)
Stilbite (aluminum)
Sugilite (aluminum)
Sulfur (toxic)
Sunstone (aluminum)
Tanzanite (aluminum)
Topaz (aluminum)
Tourmaline (aluminum)
Turquoise (copper)
Vesuvianite (aluminum)
Wavellite (aluminum)
Wulfenite (lead)
Zoisite (aluminum)

No Direct Sun	**Never Need Cleansing**
Amethyst	*Apophyllite*
Ametrine	*Auralite 23*
Blue Celestite	*Azeztulite*
Calcite	*Carnelian*
Carnelian	*Clear Quartz*
Citrine	*Diamond*
Fluorite	*Kyanite*
Opal	*Super 7*

CHAPTER TWO – Gridding

Those who dwell among the beauties and mysteries of the Earth are never alone or weary of life. – Rachel Carson

Environmental placement of gemstones

People use or are exposed to gemstones throughout our day without even realizing. Gypsum can be in the drywall surrounding us, quartz in our electronic devices, as well as minerals in our water and food. We even have crystals in our brain. Gemstones placed in our environment can reduce the electromagnetic smog, stress, negative energy and clear the air. Halite (salt) releases negative ions to cleanse the air. Black Tourmaline and Sulfur help to block negative energy. Fluorite can reduce the stress within and around us.

Our main goal in gridding or placement of stones is to connect with Earth's energy and create a healthier, more balanced work or home environment. Grid your car by placing Jet in the glove compartment to help you stay safe and accident free. Positioning Selenite in the driver's door pocket and Black Tourmaline in the passenger door pocket will protect and absorb the negativity of road rage. Yellow Obsidian will raise your vibration and lighten your mood while driving. Remember to take the stones out once a month for cleansing and recharging or place a carnelian or clear quartz with them.

Physically cleanse as well as smudge your sacred space before placing gemstones. Focus on what you want to accomplish. You can add flowers, plants, feathers, seashells, a special photograph, candles and more to enhance the intention. Place a watermelon tourmaline or green calcite near an ill plant to aid its healing. Use an elixir of rose quartz to shower it with love. Amethyst or galena water can help protect against pests. Salt lamps or halite will also keep pests away. Jade will inspire your plant to thrive and flower. Amber encourages seedlings to grow tall and strong as well as attract bees for pollination of the plant kingdom.

For prosperity and more positive energy, place a Carnelian and Sulfur by your front door. Cinnabar and Citrine can be used for prosperity as well. Place a Black Tourmaline on the right side of your front door frame and a Selenite on the left for protection in your home. You can also do this for windows. For extra protection or reduction of negativity, place a Sulfur on the window sill as well. My neighbor would disturb my sleep at 2 a.m. or 3 a.m. as he would head outside to smoke . His front door was right outside my bedroom window and his footfalls in the stairwell were loud. I had gridded the window with Selenite and Black Tourmaline when I moved in but these nighttime forays only stopped (or I stopped hearing them) once I added Sulfur.

Citrine and Carnelian can be used for energizing a space for inspiration and keeping a good work ethic. Keep Fluorite, Lapis Lazuli, Sugilite, Howlite or Aquamarine in your study space to improve concentration and instill confidence. Create a romantic atmosphere in the bedroom with Morganite or Rose Quartz. To improve sleeping, put a Rose Quartz, Amethyst, Blue Calcite, Green Calcite, or Lepidolite under your pillow or beside your head on the nightstand. You can also use these stones in a grid placing them at the corners of the bed, under the mattress or on the floor by the legs. Worries keeping you awake? Try placing a Sodalite or Selenite at the top of your head, under your pillow. Bloodstone in a clear bowl of spring water beside your head will give you a peaceful night's sleep, but only do this once a month for the full benefit of a good night's sleep as your body will get used to the vibration and won't be as effective. If you are having a problem with sleeping or insomnia, try putting an Amethyst or Lepidolite under your pillow when you go to sleep. You can also place Muscovite, Magnetite (Lodestone) or Pyrite at the head of your bed or next to it. These stones should help your body relax enough to fall asleep. If the head of your bed is in the west, and you are having trouble sleeping or staying asleep, place Selenite at the head of the bed, either on your headboard, under the mattress on the box spring or beside the bed.

Amethyst with Sulfur will protect you psychically, while Danburite will help tone down tinnitus. Danburite will also help you connect with your higher self while sleeping. If you astral travel, put a piece of Hematite or Smoky Quartz at your feet for grounding. If you need more grounding use Black Obsidian or Shiva Lingam.

Use salt lamps, Clear Quartz, Selenite, Fluorite or Amethyst near computers, microwaves, televisions and other electronic devices to purifying the air and reduce negativity. Make a gemstone elixir and spray the air to reduce negativity or illness. Geodes or cathedrals will also work to calm the atmosphere, inspire creativity, focus and decision-making. Geodes help to center yourself by balancing your chakras, clearing your mind and calming the nerves. A geode by its natural shape increases the energy of whatever gemstone it consists of and those of the gemstones that are placed within it.

You can use any gemstone for gridding or layouts – use your imagination and intuition. Know the gemstone's properties and use them in a way that is right for you. Chapter Three discusses using gemstones in a mandala, altar and medicine wheel. These are a more complex layout of gemstones but will deliver the same results.

Life changes are not easy, and we need all the help we can get trying to quit our addictions and bad habits, but in also maintaining a healthy lifestyle. Tap into the mineral kingdom to help you. Use a combination of stones to aid and strengthen your emotional, physical as well as spiritual self.

Whatever condition you want to treat, look at it from all view points. What is the emotional, the physical, the spiritual and/or the personal factor? Pick a stone to represent or take care of each of these facets of the disease. Not all crystals work with everyone the same way. Some people are more sensitive to the vibrations than others. We all have different tastes or tolerances for music, so it is with gemstones. Don't pass up a gemstone because we don't immediately resonate with it - try working with the gemstone as we many not want to face a problem or issue that it is beneficial for.

Work, home life, financial, relationship and health stress can take a toll emotionally, physically, psychologically and spiritually. People often eliminate the symptoms and not the point of stress. Perhaps we feel we cannot do anything about what is causing the stress in the first place. Maybe we feel trapped in our jobs, we can't get more money without getting another job and we don't have time for that job. Perhaps we have just had a new child or we are helping out a sick spouse or relative. We do have choices, but depending on the circumstance, we may not want to make a wrong or bad decision because someone other than ourselves may be hurt or affected. These life issues can cause a major amount of stress which may lead to disease.

After a traumatic episode, we may need psychological healing in addition to a possible physical, as well as spiritual curative. Take the case of an automobile accident in which we were the injured driver and a passenger in our car dies. Even if the accident were not our fault, we still have guilt and anguish over the death of the passenger. This is when we need to heal the whole person - emotionally, physically, psychologically and spiritually.

In the past, I would suggest one stone that would help the symptom but not address the actual issue. It would be like putting a bandage on the situation when it may need stitches to heal properly. A combination of stones should be used to address the different facets of the disease or trauma. I have intuitively combined easily available gemstones for the most common stress factors we face. I would suggest having a salt lamp (or two or three) placed in your bedroom, office or any living area where you wish to encourage peace and harmony, as well as good health, and clean the air, since it emits negative ions. Salt lamps are a natural ionizer and purifier.

Emotional trauma or stress such as grief can trigger the harshest diseases. We have to remember to treat the stress, the disease and our emotional well-being all at the same time. If we can calm our mind and disarm the stress, our bodies can heal themselves with the tools we give it such as rest, herbal teas and remedies, vitamins, minerals and nutritional foods. I will get into specific diseases and recipes further on in the book, but at this time will just address the stress part of the disease equation. Meditating with an Indicolite (Blue Tourmaline) or Apophyllite will help to reveal the cause or help with diagnosing the disease you are experiencing.

"The Crystal Bible 2" by Judy Hall has many excellent grids for you to follow for personal, spatial and spiritual situations. I use my intuition for gridding, but at times I have referenced one of Judy Hall's books for a particular grid layout when I am blocked or low on energy and can't feel what is right for me at that time.

Personal Gridding - Balancing Chakras and Reducing Stress

Personal gridding can be as easy as having stones in your pockets, wearing jewelry or placing stones in your environment. For protection, place a chunk of Sulfur on your desk or table to keep away unwanted drama or negativity. Put a piece of Selenite in the left drawer of your desk and a Black Tourmaline in your right drawer. Place them on either side of your entry door, windows or at the head and foot of the bed. You can also carry these stones in your corresponding pockets.

Here is a general idea of the stones to use for balancing your chakras. You only need one for each of the chakras. There are many chakras but I am only addressing the ones that most people recognize.

Earth/base Chakra (below feet) - Black/Brown –*Black Tourmaline (Schorl), Brown Tourmaline (Dravite), Hematite, Onyx, Obsidian, Petrified Wood, Smoky Quartz*
Ankle Chakra (Translucent Brown) - *Apache Tear, Labradorite, Smoky Quartz*
Root Chakra (Kundalini) (Red) - *Garnet, Pink Opal, Red Jasper, Ruby*
Sacral Chakra (Orange) - *Carnelian, Citrine, Orange Calcite, Tangerine Quartz, Zincite*
Solar Plexus Chakra (Yellow) - *Amber, (Yellow or Honey) Calcite, Citrine, Yellow Topaz*
Heart Chakra (Green/Pink) - *Aventurine, Bloodstone, Dioptase, Jade, Kunzite, Malachite, Morganite, Rose Quartz, Serpentine, Watermelon Tourmaline*
Throat Chakra (Light Blue) - *Blue Lace Agate, Angelite, Aquamarine, Chrysocolla, Turquoise*
Base of Brain Chakra (Medium/Dark Blue) - *Kyanite, Turquoise, Blue Fluorite, Amethyst*
Brow/Third Eye Chakra (Violet) – *Danburite, Iolite, Lapis Lazuli, Labradorite, Phenacite, Sodalite*
Crown Chakra (Violet) - *Amethyst, Charoite, Danburite, Lepidolite, Yellow Obsidian, Phenacite, Sugilite*
Higher Crown Chakra (White) - *Apophyllite, Clear Quartz, Danburite, Herkimer Diamond, Selenite*

There are many different ways to balance your chakras with gemstones: gridding by laying down and placing the stones directly on the body in the chakra positions, drinking a chakra mineral elixir, holding the gemstone that corresponds to each chakra in position in front of each chakra while meditating or by holding each gemstone in your hands in ascending order and absorbing the vibration/energy it emits, while concentrating on each individual chakra.

Since gemstones are apt to roll off when laying down, I suggest gridding in a different way by having two of each gemstone you are going to use for balancing each chakra and place them on either side of your body in ascending order in the positions of each chakra. Lying between the gemstones allows you to fully relax and not worry about the stone moving. An unconventional method, but one I have found to be extremely relaxing and more powerful, is a chakra bath.

Chakra Balancing/Cleansing Bath

Collect all gemstones that you would like to use – specifically those that correspond to each of the chakras and any you would like to use to surround you in the tub as a mandala with you in the center. If you have negativity or outside stress factors or feel as if you have hooks, attachments or darkness around you, grid the doorway (and window if you have one) with Selenite and Black Tourmaline.

Smudge all the stones, the bathtub, bathroom and yourself before starting the water. Play soft music if you wish.

Place a Clear Quartz generator or Clear Quartz tumbled stones in each of the corners of the tub. If you wish, you can also use Rose Quartz, Amethyst, Carnelian with a Clear Quartz for the corners of the tub to balance the metaphysically/spiritual and emotional bodies. Go with what feels right to you.

Place a Rose Quartz in the middle of the tub (if you don't put it in the corners of the tub), as you are filling up the bath with water. You want to be surrounded by unconditional love. (If you wish to use essential oils, Himalayan salt, homemade bath salts - baking soda and sea salt with essential oils - or Epsom salt, add them after the Rose Quartz).

Once the bathtub is to the level you desire, shut off the water and gently climb into the tub. If you are physically able, kneel with your face just above the water. Ask Creator (Spirit, God, Allah, Christ, Ascended Masters, Angels) to bless and protect you. Ask that your guides, guardians, angels and light beings protect and surround you with light. Gently ease your face into the water and bend your knees into a crouching position as in prayer. Pray briefly if you so wish and then bring your head back up. Slowly turn and sit in the tub, making sure you have moved the Rose Quartz out of the way, but leaving it in the water at your feet.

Start with a meditation chant that is comfortable for you or just say "Only Love and Light Lives Here, Only Love and Light is Allowed" four times. As you are saying this aloud, or to yourself, set the intention of the bath and what you wish to receive from it: healing, chakra balancing, stress removal, inner peace or a combination of these. Accept all parts of yourself, good and bad – physical, emotional, intellectual and spiritual. Do not judge looks or feelings, allow the process and relax.

Example of a healing and balancing bath

Starting with a Clear Quartz crystal, hold it in your hands and see yourself relaxing and clearing your mind. Just quietly breathe in and out and feel the peace.

Once you feel comfortable, place the Clear Quartz crystal in front of the Rose Quartz crystal, away from you, in a line. Starting with the base chakra, pick up the gemstone that you wish to use to represent that chakra. I use Red Jasper. Holding the Red Jasper in your hands, focus on your base chakra and feel the energy of the stone (or direct the energy of the stone) to that chakra. Ask the stone for healing and balance. After a few minutes or when you feel ready, put the stone into the water between your feet at the farthest point from you.

Pick up a Carnelian stone (or whichever stone you are using for the sacral chakra).

Hold it in your hands and focus on the sacral chakra. Ask the stone for healing and balancing. When ready, place the stone into the water in front of the root chakra stone (or coming toward you).

Pick up your Citrine stone (or whichever stone you are using for the solar plexus). Hold it in your hands, and focus on your solar plexus. Breathe in deeply and exhale even more deeply – pushing out all of your breath that you can, envisioning all the negativity and darkness leaving your body. Do this three more times for a total of four times. On the last exhale, breathe in slowly and easily, envisioning clear healing light entering your body and expanding your lungs. Place the stone in the water in front of the sacral chakra heading toward you. Continue to place each of the following stones in a line getting close to you or to the Rose Quartz and Clear Quartz.

Use Bloodstone or another stone for your heart chakra, holding it in your hands and asking for healing and balancing of that chakra. If you are going through emotional trauma such as a break up, argument with your spouse or a friend, grieving for a loved one, etc., take your time on this chakra; take as long as necessary to feel calm. Let the tears flow if that is how you feel. Allow this chakra to cleanse, heal and release all that does not serve you.

When you are ready, move onto a Blue Lace Agate for your throat chakra or use another stone for communication. Ask for healing and balancing of that chakra. If you are a person who has a hard time speaking up for yourself, allow yourself a little more time working on this chakra. Walk your talk, and talk your walk!

Continue to heal and balance your chakras using an Iolite for the third eye. I also used a Rhodochrosite for my ears to increase my psychic hearing and clear communication or reception of messages.

Use an Amethyst for your crown chakra and envision this stone's purple ray filtering throughout your whole body bringing healing, de-stressing and allow inner peace. When you are ready, pick up the Clear Quartz stone at the base of the Rose Quartz and continue your healing and envision a white light surrounding your body, as well as filtering through it and out your feet. Feel the energy in the water as well as around you. Feel the power of the stones within as without.

If you have a laser quartz point, this would be the time to use it for specific healing points in your body, such as eyes, ears, heart, joints, etc. Use the laser point on each area you wish to heal, aid or strengthen.

If you have negative people, grief, or gone through a breakup, use the laser quartz to remove any hooks or ties. See your laser pointer cutting the ties that bind and melting any hooks that others have in you. Pass the laser point down along the front of your body from the crown chakra to your feet and see all that holds you back as cut or melting away from you. Do this three times, and at the end of the third time, allow the laser pointer to be rinsed in the bath water. Bring the pointer back up to your crown chakra and as you pass it down the front of your body, envision is it actually going down your back and cutting ties or melting the hooks there as well. Do this three times, and cleanse the laser in the water.

At this point, you should be extremely relaxed and feeling more positive.

Be aware of your feelings toward your body, your spirit, your intellect and your emotions. If they are not in harmony, work with the stones that will help to bring you into balance. You can combine the stones as necessary – such as heart and sacral chakra if you have physical and emotional trauma from a spouse, co-worker or ex. Use the root and solar plexus stones for physical healing of trauma to your legs or trunk of your body. Whatever you have sent the intention for this bath, make sure you have accomplished your goal and feel calm.

Remove the stones from the water in reverse order of use and place on the side of the tub. As you start to drain the tub, feel all the negativity and darkness being pulled out of your body at your feet and going down the drain. Before the tub is completely empty, stand up in the tub and allow the last part of the water to pull at your feet as it drains out. Take a shower with organic soap and cleanse yourself from head to toe to remove any last vestiges of negativity.

Once you are done with the shower, smudge your body once again to renew, protect and thank the Creator and all your light beings. Be sure to drink lots of water to help in purifying yourself and to continue flushing out the negativity or disease. Smudge/cleanse the stones you have used and recharge them.

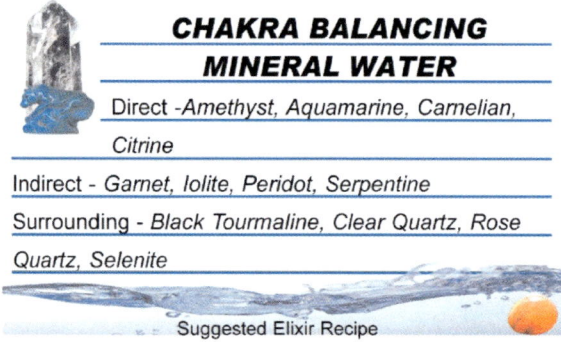

CHAKRA BALANCING MINERAL WATER

Direct - *Amethyst, Aquamarine, Carnelian, Citrine*

Indirect - *Garnet, Iolite, Peridot, Serpentine*

Surrounding - *Black Tourmaline, Clear Quartz, Rose Quartz, Selenite*

Suggested Elixir Recipe

CHAPTER THREE – Mandalas, Altars and Medicine Wheels

"In a crystal we have clear evidence of the existence of a formative life principle, and though we cannot understand the life of a crystal, it is nonetheless a living being." -Nikola Tesla

De-stressing Environmentally, Emotionally And Spiritually

Meditation is one way to de-stress but, if you are like me, it is almost impossible to quiet the mind. I tried different techniques and was not been very successful until I started meditating with crystals. If there is an activity that you really enjoy and get into such as gardening, that can be a form of meditation. When alone with our thoughts while driving, cleaning, gardening, listening to music, etc., we go into a relaxed state similar to that of meditation and self-realization. Help yourself to attain this state by building a mandala or altar of gemstones to aid you.

Working with the gemstones to create a mandala or altar is a form of meditation and clears the mind, heart and soul, bringing inner peace. The gemstones you choose should resonate with you and chosen by instinct. If you have a specific goal in mind, then choose gemstones that support that intention. It is okay to look the up stones' properties that you want to use in a book, but as you get more comfortable and familiar with the stones, use your intuition and let your feelings guide you. Feel free to play soft, spiritual music as you create.

Mandala. A mandala is a symbol, diagram, chart, or geometric pattern which represents the universe in a metaphysical or spiritual way. Traditionally used by Indian religions to represent the universe.

Altar. An altar is a flat-topped table or surface used as the focus for a religious ritual or prayer.

Mandalas and altars are used for the highest good. Using gemstones is a personal choice. Deciding which gemstones to use is best defined by your intention. Do you wish to raise your vibration and connect better with the Divine, do you want to sending healing energy to others as well as yourself, or would you like to manifest a better way of life? Think about the gemstone shapes and colors you want to use in relation to your intention. Pyramids, generators, spheres, points, tumbled raw pieces can give it more meaning, instill a sense of urgency or pinpoint an issue, or exude a soft, calming influence.

If you wish to raise your vibration and meditate, create a mandala or altar with gemstones such as Angelite, Apophyllite, Blue Celestite, Clear Quartz, Super Seven, Auralite23, Moldavite, Danburite, Amethyst, Citrine, Herkimer Diamond, Hiddenite, Kunzite, Petalite and Azeztulite are a few you can use.

Surround these with protecting crystals such as Smoky Quartz, Hematite, Black Tourmaline, Selenite, Sulfur or Jasper. Add some love or emotionally uplifting crystals such as Rose Quartz, Morganite, Yellow Obsidian, Dioptase, Emerald or Larimar. If you have a tendency to "drift off" or become lightheaded during meditation, using grounding stones such as Hematite, boji stones, chrysanthemum stone, shiva lingham, lodestone or granite. Surrounding or incorporate Clear Quartz to boost the energy to any layout.

Perhaps you have writer's block, or you are an artist in need of an idea for a new painting or creation. Use stones that will enhance your creativity or inspire. Use manifesting or artistic stones, such as Amazonite, Amber, Amethyst Spirit Quartz, Aqua Aura, Aquamarine,

Blue Aragonite, Blue Celestite, Blue Fluorite, Citrine, Clear Quartz, Garnet, Kunzite, Magnesite, Mookaite, Morganite, Peacock Stone, Rainbow Jasper, Staurolite, Tangerine Quartz or Zincite. Just open yourself up to whatever attracts your attention or stirs your emotions. This is your world, your personal mandala or altar and whatever you choose will be right for you.

Creating A Mandala for Inner Peace and De-Stressing

When creating a mandala, you work in circles and layers to achieve an aesthetically, emotionally as well spiritually, pleasing experience. You can use all different shapes, sizes, colors and textures of minerals to create your vision of the universe or visual prayer manifestation. Think of it as painting with gemstones. If you are making a gemstone mandala to represent love, you could use Morganite, Rose Quartz, Selenite, Larimar and other stones that remind you of this emotion. Before building your mandala, I suggest smudging yourself and all the stones to purify yourself and your intentions.

To create a mandala for inner peace or to de-stress, place an Aquamarine or Pink Tourmaline in the center of the surface you are using. This stone represents you and what you want to achieve or manifest. Surround this stone with four amethyst points facing away from the stone at the 3, 6, 9 and 12 positions of a clock. This symbolizes the release of stress and all that doesn't serve you. Make the next circle of stones with 8 citrine points facing inward. This symbolizes the manifestation of peace and abundance. Make the next circle of stones with 8 amethyst stones (if points face them inward) or fluorite stones and four Rose Quartz stones at the 3, 6, 9 and 12 positions. This represents emotional health, harmony and spiritual enlightenment. Make an outer circle of stones with Angelite, Clear Quartz, Apophyllite, Rose Quartz, Danburite and other high-vibration stones. This represents your Higher Self, the Angelic Realm and the Creator. Outside this circle place protection and negativity reducing stones such as Selenite, Black Tourmaline, Hematite, Sulfur and Amethyst.

If you don't have these specific stones, then use the stones you have that represent what you are trying to achieve. There is no right or wrong way – just your way. If you don't get the desired effect you are trying to achieve, then experiment with other stones of a higher or lower vibration until you "feel" that it is right for you aesthetically, emotionally and spiritually.

Creating An Altar

For me, the main difference between a mandala and an altar is when creating an altar, I make the altar more personal and keyed to me instead of to another or geared toward the universe. This is your prayer or sacred space and should reflect your inner being and what you are trying to manifest. Personalize your gemstone altar with things that touch your emotions, such as feathers, seashells, animal totems, angel statues, crosses, stars, rosary beads, candles or pictures of ascended masters, guides or the Creator. Pull from your own ethnic, religious or geographic preferences. Incorporate the elements, directions, the moon and/or sun. This altar is your own creation for personal prayer or ceremonies. It is for the highest good - make sure when building it that your intention is from the Light.

Before building your altar, I suggest smudging yourself and all the materials you wish to use in order to purify yourself and set your intentions more solidly. Starting in the middle of your altar space, place a stone, feather, picture, candle or whatever you believe to represent yourself or what you are trying to achieve. An altar does not have to consist of circles within circles. It can be laid out in a cross, pyramid, 'X' pattern, semi-circle, arch or whatever pattern is meaningful to you.

If you have a cathedral, salt lamp or other extremely large stone that you want to use for your altar, place it in the back of the stones and materials you are going to use. If you find gardening a peaceful experience, perhaps add a small plant on the edge of your altar. Or maybe make an outdoor medicine wheel/altar in your garden.

When using large candles, place them in the back or to the sides of the altar you are going to build. You can start with these or end with them, whatever feels right in your ritual or ceremony. You can start your prayers before building an altar, while building the altar and incorporating each piece and/or after the altar is completed. This is entirely up to you.

A sample altar to bring inner peace could be a small white candle in the middle of the altar to represent you and your purified intentions in your prayer. You could place some Manifestation Crystals, Quartz Generators or Rose Quartz stones around the candle in a line diamond, square, cross, circle or directional placement. Use as many or as few stones as you wish. Incorporate some Fluorite, Selenite, Amazonite, Aquamarine, Scolecite, Pink Tourmaline and/or Carnelian into your altar. Place some seashells or coral on the altar if you find tranquility at the ocean or some pinecones, acorns, leaves or small twigs if you like to walk in the forest. If you follow some indigenous rituals, perhaps make your altar more of a medicine or energy wheel and add feathers, totem items, sacred herbs, cornmeal or sage, cedar and sweetgrass.

Personal Medicine Wheel Altar for Balance and Decision Making

When you are trying to find your path or diagnose your emotional, spiritual or physical disease, it can be helpful to meditate with stones laid out in a personal medicine wheel. This layout may help you to make decisions that are for your highest good and in a rational manner. Starting with the center, choose a stone or item that will represent yourself or how you see yourself. Working in a circular motion and starting in the East or Earth position (at the 3:00 position), select a personal stone that reflects your intention. This is the basis of your meditation or questioning. Pick stones that you are drawn to. (Petrified Wood would be a good stone to use for rebirth or new beginnings. Lapis Lazuli would work for physical trauma. Choose an Amazonite for new ventures. Select a Fluorite for stress and earthly worries. Place a

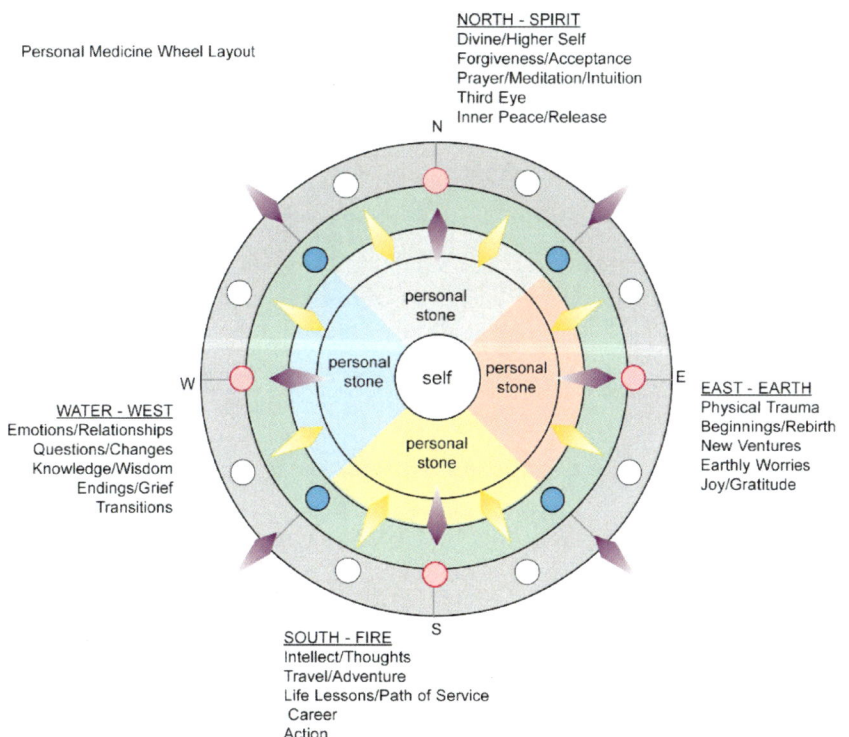

Kunzite for joy and gratitude.)

    Moving on to the South position or Fire, choose your next stone based on what you would like to explore. (Sugilite or Howlite would be good for working on intellect/thought questioning. Sodalite is the gemstone for travel or Azeztulite for adventure. Use Charoite to discover your path of service and life lessons. Amazonite will help find your career or creativity. Carnelian or Zincite will help you to discern what action to take.)

    In the West or Water position, choose stones to help with your emotional issues. (Rhodochrosite works on the child within while Rose Quartz bring unconditional love and safety. Have to make a decision- choose Blue Celestite or Clear Quartz for clarity and bring through the wisdom or knowledge you are seeking. Chiastolite will aid in releasing grief. Aquamarine will help you release your anger, frustration or hurt feelings when dealing with an ending or new life path. Moonstone aids with changes or transitions.)

    The North is our spiritual center and helps us define what is for our highest good. (Use Danburite or Apophyllite to connect with the Divine, your Higher Self, Guides and/or Angels. Dioptase allows us to forgive and move forward. Cinnabar aids with acceptance and serenity. Clear Quartz and Amethyst aid with meditation, Fugilite with prayer and Labradorite or Lapis Lazuli with intuition. Iolite will balance and open your third eye. Pink Tourmaline grants inner peace, while Aquamarine allows you to release all your worldly troubles for a time.)

    Position Amethyst points away from the center at the 3, 6, 9 and 12 o'clock positions to remove all that is unwanted. Use Citrine points facing inward between the Amethyst points to bring blessings, healing and to help manifest your desires. Place Turquoise around the wheel to remove negativity, add protection and to bring all the pieces together to work toward wholeness/wellness. Place Rose Quartz at the 3, 6, 9 and 12 o'clock positions to bring the feeling of unconditional love and acceptance. Make a ring of Clear Quartz around the outside perimeter for protection, to enhance the energy of all the stones and to provide clarity in your meditation. You can also place Amethyst points facing inward to enhance your intuition and reception of any spiritual messages or gifts.

    Personalize the outside of the medicine wheel with pictures, feathers, herbs, plants, shells, candles or other gemstones that pertain to your meditation or to aid in bringing about whatever resolution you are looking for and that is for your highest good. Things don't always come to us in the way we wish or understand but always work out in our best interest and in the interest of those around us.

CHAPTER FOUR – Making Elixirs

"A diamond is merely a lump of coal that is made good under pressure." – Henry Kissinger

Holistic Health is about looking at the whole person, not just the symptoms. It includes the energy and spiritual bodies and power centers (or the chakras), as well as the physical body. Removing the symptoms does not always remove the problem or the root cause of the condition. Sometimes, we must look deeper and use our intuition. Let's first start by gathering as much information as possible. Write down whatever comes to you as you think about what you are trying to accomplish.

1. What is the problem and what might have caused the problem? (Injury, diet, accident, etc.)
2. Medical history? (Allergies, surgery, genetics etc.) Do you smoke/drink/take recreation or prescription drugs?
3. Undergoing any treatments, and if so, for what? (Energy healing, acupuncture, radiation, etc.)
4. Women – Are you pregnant or having your menstrual cycle?
5. What are your habits? (Diet, exercise, sleep)
6. Any physical indicators such as swelling/inflammation, bruising, rapid pulse, temperature, etc?
7. Emotional factors (childhood issues, trauma, abuse, bullying, low self-esteem, accident, guilt, etc.)

Before making an elixir, you should have done your research or tapped into your bodies to discover more about the disease or are experiencing and tried to find the root cause behind the symptoms. It can be as simple as a tension headache or the headache could be a reaction to medication, stress or caffeine withdrawal. Or perhaps you were in a car accident, have allergies or some other traumatic experience. Once you have seen a doctor for anything that appears to be serious, then you can work with the mineral kingdom to help your body heal itself.

Experiment by holding certain gemstones and feeling their energy to see how they affect the disease. Five to 10 minutes is all you need to know if the gemstone is going to help. As you work with gemstones over a period of time, you will intuitively pick the stones more quickly. Sometimes I don't have the stone I need with me, but having worked with gemstones for years, I just have to visualize the gemstone I want to use and my body automatically keys to the vibration of the stone by memory and aids my body in healing itself.

There are several different things to consider when making your elixir. Will the stone(s) be used in the direct/indirect method, left in the refrigerator or charged with sunlight or moonlight, and what surrounds the bowl, i.e., where will it be placed and will you use candles, feathers, shells, angel statues, music, other crystals, etc. Will this be used right away or saved as a tincture?

Direct/Indirect Method – Depending on the properties of the gemstone is how you will use them directly or indirectly. Any raw, fragile, water soluble, metallic (such as aluminum, lead, copper, etc) or Sulfur containing gemstones should be used indirectly.

Sunlight/Moonlight – Rule of thumb when putting your elixir in sunlight or moonlight – you get a higher energy in sunlight and a more calming energy with moonlight. When you do both sunlight and moonlight you balance the energy in the elixir. If battling depression, make sure to use sunlight to give more positive, uplifting energy to the mineral water as the full moon could deepen a depression.

Remember to consider the weather – is it sunny, cloudy or rainy? A cloudy or rainy day will not have as much sunlight during the day and may be better for those who have a high energy level to begin with.

Or if you are prone to depression or have a hard time getting up and going, you would want a higher energy elixir, so you would have no moonlight and all sunlight. Bipolar disorder elixirs should be balanced and both moonlight and sunlight would be used. Consider the moon cycles if keeping the elixir in the sun and moonlight for a day or more. (Never go more than three days.) Full moon will give more energy and add to an elixir, while a new moon will extract unnecessary elements or energy. Female energy (softer) would be moonlight, while sunlight (more powerful) is male energy. A few examples of elixirs that you would use in a new moon would be those for addictions, bad habits, tumors and bone spurs. Fertility elixirs would be made during a full moon for the most potent moon energy, while virility elixirs would be made during a new moon.

Once you have decided what you are using, where it will be placed, and have all the necessary ingredients, it is time to begin. You will need a clear glass bowl; a small clear glass bowl, shot glass, or other clear glass container to place inside the larger bowl; spring, distilled or mineral water; appropriate gemstones; a table or tray or place that you will be able to leave your elixir in the sunlight/moonlight undisturbed (if outside, use clear plastic wrap to keep clean); vodka, brandy or cider vinegar; and any special colors, candles, seashells, feathers, etc. If you are just making a regular elixir of one or two gemstones and are not concerned about the weather, sunlight, moonlight (and you need it immediately), then you may just make an elixir overnight in the refrigerator. I recommend a minimum of three hours, but it is best when the gemstones soak for six hours or more.

To make a stronger more personalized elixir, start with a cleansing/smudging ritual for yourself and all the equipment, stones, etc., you will be using. Take a few minutes to meditate, first by yourself and then with the gemstones you will use. With each gemstone, set an intention of what you want it to do – this will only take about 10 seconds for each stone. Envision healing light surrounding the gemstone and then place it accordingly, either in the spring water directly, in a containment bowl within the spring water, or on the outside of the bowl as a mandala, medicine wheel or grid layout. Invite the Divine to bless your elixir in whatever way you wish. (A few times I have made elixirs and the mineral water had the smell of roses but not the taste. I truly believe these elixirs were blessed by Spirit/Creator/Angels/The Divine.)

Leave the elixir undisturbed for 6-24 hours depending on your intention. If you are/charging the infusion with sunlight, make it in the morning and it will be ready by sundown. If moonlight, make it at dusk and it will be ready by sunrise. If you are using both sunlight and moonlight, make sure you leave it for 24 hours. A new moon or full moon energy can be used three nights – the day before the full or new moon, the actual day and the day after. When using only new moon or full moon energy, be sure you take your bowl out of the sunlight during the day or covering it up with a towel.

Once the elixir is ready – and you are making it as a tincture - pour the elixir into a dark glass bottle, adding a dropper-full of vodka, brandy or cider vinegar. This method works for sprays, skin applications or to be ingested at regular intervals. If you don't like putting anything into the elixir, then store it in the refrigerator for up to three months. This is called a "mother" tincture and you use it by the dropper, teaspoon, tablespoon or jigger. You can add this mother tincture to your water, tea, cooking, baking, bath water, other elixirs, etc. If you make a mother tincture of individual stones, don't hesitate to combine these mother tinctures to make your own recipe or to merge them for one of the recipes in this book. The recipes I have created can be adapted by changing out one or two stones for ones you feel will work best for you, or if you wish, you may want to use just the direct/indirect method without using any surrounding stones. You don't have to use all the stones I have listed in the recipes, or you may substitute

Clear Quartz to take the place of a stone you may not have in your collection. Clear Quartz can be programmed to have the properties of any stone you need.

As I have already stated, stress is one of the major contributors to disease. The rest of this book will be dedicated to recipes and gemstone suggestions for specific conditions but this chapter will deal with the many causes of stress and elixir recipes to treat them.

There are many stones that you can use but the recipes I have created/intuited use easily acquired gemstones. There are a few cases where I have listed one or two more rare stones, but there will always be another stone or combination that can be used in their stead. You also can program clear quartz to be any other stone. Some general stones to use for stress are Fluorite, Morganite, Amber, Aragonite, Amethyst, Azurite, Green Calcite, Aquamarine, Scolecite and Blue Celestite (Angelite). These can be worn as jewelry, kept in pockets, under your pillow, beside your computer, in your desk drawer, or as an elixir that you can add to your tea, coffee, water or take by dropper. Use them as surrounding stones when making your elixirs to reduce strain, nervousness and stress.

Destressing with Gemstone Elixirs
P - physical, EN-energetic, EM- emotional, IN- intellectual & S- spiritual metaphysical properties

JOB STRESS

Anyone who works can relate to this subject. Even if you love your job, there is a co-worker, client, or project that can cause anxiety and stress. Select the gemstones that best represent the kind of stress you are experiencing. Keep them in your pockets, on your desk or add some of the elixir to your drinks to aid you in combating this type of stress. Children going to school, studying and/or taking tests can feel the same type of stress as adults.

Amber – (P)(EM)(EN)(IN) Promotes positive mental state and patience, calming influence, mood uplifter, memory aid
Amethyst – (P)(EN)(EM)(IN)(S) Mind, body and spirit balance, calms thoughts, nerves, encourages harmony and cooperation
Apophyllite – (P)(EN)(IN)(S) Relieves stress, releases negative thought process, re-energizes, spiritual attunement and support, work together as a group,
Aquamarine – (P)(EM)(EN)(IN) Tolerance of others, reduces stress, calms mind, courage, instills responsibility and organization, promotes self-expression and communication
Auralite 23 – (P)(EN)(EM)(IN)(S) Calms nerves, relaxes anxiety, boosts energy, can-do attitude
Blue Lace Agate – (P)(EN)(EM)(IN) Clear communication, calms, peace of mind, neutralizes anger
Carnelian – (P)(EN)(EM)(IN)(S) Harmony, motivation, stimulates creativity, motivates for success in business, builds courage, improves analytical abilities, sharpens concentration
Chiastolite – (EN)(EM) Transmutes conflict into harmony, dispels negative thoughts/feelings, calms fears
Citrine – (EN)(EM)(IN) Abundance, harmonizes group discord, success, self-confidence
Clear Quartz – (EN)(IN)(S) Purification, clarity of thought, protection and energy booster, works for highest good
Fluorite – (P)(EN)(S) Protection, calms, repels negativity, organizes, purifies, overcomes chaos, balances on all levels
Jade – (EM)(EN)(IN)(S) Insight, simplifies tasks and ideas, calms, prosperity, creativity, good health

Jasper – (EM)(EN)(IN) Determination, support in conflicts, assertiveness, quick thinking and decision making, organization, stability

Kyanite – (P)(EM)(EN)(IN)(S) Bring peace of mind, compassion, boost decision making and logical thoughts, aids with communication and organization, release of fears and negativity

Labradorite – (P)(EM)(EN)(IN)(S) – Calms anger, reduces stress, supports intelligent decisions, instills optimism and hope

Lepidolite – (P)(EM)(EN) Peaceful night sleep, calms/soothes nerves, realization of one's goals/dreams, acceptance of change

Magnesite – (P)(EM) Relieves tension/stress, reduces headaches, aids clear thoughts and decision making

Rose Quartz – (EM) Unconditional love, infinite peace, harmony, trust, acceptance of change

Sardonyx – (P)(EM)(EN)(IN) Builds willpower, self-control, stamina, aids in decision making, promotes financial independence

Scolecite – (EM)(EN)(S) Peacefulness, opens paths of communication, team spirit and cooperation

Shungite – (P)(EN)(EM)(IN)(S) Instill peace, calms nerves, reduces negative energy, reduces chaos, encourages organization and responsibility, protects you from electro-magnetic emissions

Sulfur – (EN) Transmutes and blocks negativity, calms anger, promotes clear thinking and harmony, acceptance of what you cannot change

Sunstone – (P)(EM)(EN) Instills a take charge attitude and faith in oneself, nurturing, renews joy of life, battles procrastination

Tiger Iron – (P)(EM)(IN) Emotional and mental burnout, aids in adapting to changes, pragmatic decisions and solution

Turitella Agate – (P)(EM) Support in transitions, reduces stress, acceptance, calms stomach, work toward one's dream/goals

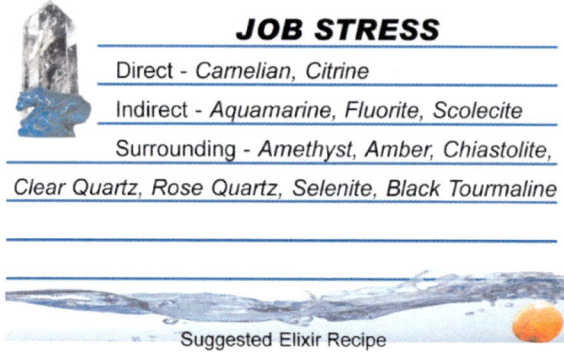

JOB STRESS
Direct - *Carnelian, Citrine*
Indirect - *Aquamarine, Fluorite, Scolecite*
Surrounding - *Amethyst, Amber, Chiastolite, Clear Quartz, Rose Quartz, Selenite, Black Tourmaline*

Suggested Elixir Recipe

FINANCIAL STRESS

These days, who doesn't have financial stress? Even if you are a millionaire or billionaire, you still have financial worries. Do I have enough money to cover my bills, my retirement, my family's needs, college tuition, health insurance or medical bills, vehicle costs, etc.? Make an elixir to aid with the loss of a job, getting a new job that will pay more, change part-time to full-time employment, new investments or projects, new or old business anxieties and more. Financial stress can go hand in hand with job stress, and you will see some of the stones here are similar to those for job stress. Don't be afraid to combine elixirs for different problems or stressful situations that are unique to you.

Ametrine – (P)(EN)(EM)(IN)(S) Combination of the characteristics of Amethyst and Citrine
Amethyst – (P)(EN)(EM)(IN)(S) Transmutes negative, instills self worth, harmonizes thoughts, emotions and actions, prosperity in business
Apache Tear – (EM)(EN)(IN)(S) Transmutes negativity, removes self-limitations, aid insight, calm stress
Aventurine – (EM)(EN)(IN) Instills responsibility, leadership and decision making, turning intelligent ideas into action
Bixbite – (P)(EM)(EN)(IN) Courage, relieves stress, energizes, positive view if discouraged
Blue Fluorite – (EM)(EN)(IN) New perspectives and ideas for making ends meet, refocus and plan, creative resolutions, calms worries, aids in looking beyond moment, shows possibilities in distant places
Carnelian – (P)(EN) EM)(IN)(S) Harmony, motivation, stimulates creativity, motivates for success in business, builds courage, improves analytical abilities, sharpens concentration
Chalcedony – (P)(EM)(IN) Strength, resourcefulness, persistence to attain goals
Cinnabar – (P)(EN)(IN) Attracts abundance, assertiveness in selling without aggression, organization, success in projects
Citrine – (P)(EM)(EN)(IN)(S) Creates, manifests, attracts wealth, prosperity, success, happiness, hold onto what you have, self-confidence
Diamond – (P)(EN) Attracts abundance and wealth, enhances energy
Emerald – (P)(EM)(EN)(IN)(S) Strength, wisdom, recovery and regeneration
Garnet – (P)(EM) Passion, stone of plenty, encouragement, hope, amplifies other crystals energies
Jade – (EM)(EN)(IN) Good health, good luck, wisdom, promotes self sufficiency, insight and ideas
Kyanite – (P)(EM)(EN)(IN)(S) Boost decision making and logical thoughts, aids with communication and organization, release of fears and negativity allowing one increase one's finances with stability
Kunzite/Hiddenite – (EN)(S) See blessings you have and recognize those that you will soon come across
Labradorite – (P)(EM)(EN)(IN)(S) – Calms anger, instills optimism/hope, larger perspective, new ideas
Phenacite – (EN)(S) Release things to a higher power, brings a higher perspective
Sardonyx – (P)(EM)(EN)(IN) Builds willpower, self-control, stamina, aids in decision making, promotes financial independence
Sunstone – (P)(EM)(EN)(IN) Instills a take charge attitude and faith in oneself, nurturing, renews joy of life, battles procrastination

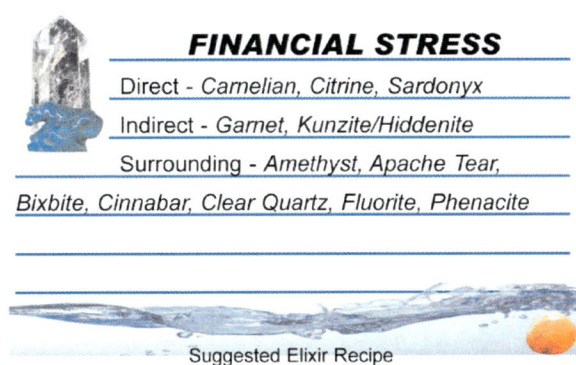

FINANCIAL STRESS
Direct - *Carnelian, Citrine, Sardonyx*
Indirect - *Garnet, Kunzite/Hiddenite*
Surrounding - *Amethyst, Apache Tear, Bixbite, Cinnabar, Clear Quartz, Fluorite, Phenacite*

Suggested Elixir Recipe

RELATIONSHIPS

A relationship is not just between two or more people, family members or co-workers, it is also with oneself. A relationship exists between you and your pets, your plants, your spiritual guides, guardians, angels or anything you may have a passion or feeling toward. Relationships can be positive or negative, in the present, past or wishes for the future. You cannot change anyone else, but you can change your perspective, tolerance and understanding of situations to make better decisions when it comes to working together, finding love, increasing happiness or learning to accept and love yourself. Gemstones will aid you in finding the courage, strength and wisdom to know when to hang in a situation or relationship or if it is better to leave. They help you to clarify your thoughts, emotions and spiritual guidance to act for your highest good.

Agate – (P)(EM)(EN)(I)(S) Heals past hurts, open heart, balances emotional, physical and intellectual bodies, reduces anger and tension, builds on a forever relationship and commitment

Albite – (EM)(EN) – Encourages cooperation, tact, "go with the flow" attitude, clarity of thought, self confidence, commitment, personal growth and change within a relationship

Ametrine – (P)(EM)(EN)(IN)(S) Bringing opposing viewpoints and thoughts into harmony, enhances communication, clarifies what is best for all in decision making, brings intellectual and emotional into balance, aids in rebuilding trust

Amethyst – (P)(EM)(EN)(IN)(S) Healing past, moving forward, turns focus on most important attributes, decision making, balances feelings, equalizes highs and lows

Apache Tear – (P)(EM)(EN)(IN)(S) Release of grief and negative emotions, past traumas, nightmares, brings new love

Aquamarine – (EM)(EN)(S) Release of emotions in a healthy and safe way, instills a feeling of peace and safety, promotes healing in the grieving process, aids with closure of past relationships and moving forward, tolerance and clear, concise communication

Auralite 23 – (P)(EN)(EM)(IN)(S) Calms nerves, relaxes anxiety, boosts insight and energy, can-do attitude, release anger and past hurt, focuses on positive present and future, larger perspective, tolerance and understanding

Aventurine – (P)(EM)(EN)(IN)(S) Healing the heart, opening to new love, taking responsibility for past actions and decisions, seeing your part in past relationships and moving forward in better patterns, being more aware of your impact upon others emotions and lives

Azeztulite – (P)(EM)(EN)(IN)(S) Supports a loving environment, release of grudges, shows the "cancer" in relationship and allows one to make decision to hold on and fight or cut it loose, instills a sense of higher self, humility, sense of service to others, greater connection to all living beings and universal love

Azurite – (EM)(IN)(S) Harmony of intellect and heart, balances emotions, aids in dissolving conflict and arguments, instills compassion and understanding

Blue Lace Agate – (EM)(IN) Clear communication, calms anger, brings up feelings and allows for expression without judgment

Brown Tourmaline – (EM)(EN)(S) Removes negativity, increases libido, removes sexual emotional dysfunction, aids in understanding oneself and others, boosts empathy and compassion

Carnelian – (EM)(IN)(S) Instills a sense of harmony, positive life choices, motivates for success, promotes trust and loyalty, working together as one unit

Chiastolite – (EN)(EM) Changes conflict into harmony, dispel negative thoughts and feelings, calms fears, brings comfort to grief-stricken or transitioning souls and their loved ones, releases feelings of guilt

Chrysoprase – (EM)(EN)(S) Calms anger and helps hold back harmful words, encourages healing in trust issues, forgiveness, balances emotions, acccptance of own and others limitations, encourages understanding and compassion for self and others

Clear Quartz – (P)(EN)(IN)(S) Clarity of thoughts and situations, healing energy, removes blockages, enhance energy of othcr crystals

Dioptase – (EM)(S) Forgiveness of oneself and others, aids in emotional healing from betrayal and heartache, relieves grief

Emerald – (P)(EM)(EN)(IN)(S) Domestic bliss, successful partnership, enhances friendship, unconditional love, commitment, loyalty, eliminates negativity

Kyanite – (P)(EM)(EN)(IN)(S) Bring peace of mind, compassion, aids with communication and organization, release of fears and negativity, creative problem solving

Larimar – (P)(EM)(EN)(IN)(S) Nurturing of self and others, love, peace, tranquility, promotes loyalty, taking control of life, alleviating guilt, fear of new situations, reinforces feelings of joy and playfulness

Malachite – (EM)(EN)(IN) Personal will, standing up for self in positive, non-aggressive way, clarifying emotions/feelings for another

Moonstone – (EM)(EN)(S) – Personal strength and empowerment, learns everything is a cycle, relaxes and calms fears, strengthens bonds with children

Morganite – (P)(EM)(EN)(IN)(S) Enhances and attracts love in thought, action and emotion, calms stress, opens heart and mind, heals soul, recognize/shed baggage, teaches to view things with an open mind and in a positive light

Orange Calcite – (P)(EM)(EN) Mood uplifter, restores optimism, spontaneity, self love, child-like wonder, peaceful feelings toward others, playfulness in life, love and sex, confidence

Rhodochrosite – (P)(EM)(EN)(S) Protection, healing of childhood and emotional traumas, sexual abuse, reawakening the inner child, reconnection, optimism, self-love

Rhodonite – (P)(EM)(EN)(IN)(S) Balances emotions, encourages love, heals emotional trauma and aids with forgiveness, defeats self-destruction and instills self-confidence, respect and love

Rose Quartz – (EM)(EN)(S) Unconditional love for self and others, empathy

Shungite – (P)(EN)(EM)(IN)(S) Instill peace, calms nerves, reduces negative energy, reduces chaos, encourages organization and responsibility, supports caregivers physically and emotionally with positive energy which in turn allows the caregiver to be more patient, understanding to aid the individual as well as self in healing

Sunstone – (P)(EM)(EN)(IN) Instills a take charge attitude and faith in oneself, nurturing, aids in releasing the "ties that bind

Tangerine Quartz – (EM)(EN) Releases negative emotions, restores balance in feelings, promotes optimism and better outlook, removes feelings of loneliness, being alone, give strength to willpower and courage to stand up for oneself

Tiger Iron – (EM)(EN)(IN) Family stress, adapting to change, finding common ground, a safe haven

Topaz – (P)(EM)(EN)(IN)(S) Calms stress and nerves, creates mellow mood, promotes forgiveness, encourages truth/honesty, increases bonds of friendship and love, instills self-confidence and self-worth

RELATIONSHIP STRESS
Creating Harmony/Reducing Stress
Direct - *Aquamarine, Blue Lace Agate, Carnelian, Larimar*
Indirect - *Tiger Iron, Dioptase*
Surrounding - *Amethyst, Brown Tourmaline, Chrysoprase, Clear Quartz, Rose Quartz*
Suggested Elixir Recipe

RELATIONSHIP STRESS
Calming Anger/Releasing Negative Emotions
Direct - *Amethyst, Blue Lace Agate, Rose Quartz, Shungite*
Indirect - *Chiastolite, Orange Calcite, Kyanite*
Surrounding - *Azeztulite, Clear Quartz, Selenite, Sunstone*
Suggested Elixir Recipe

RELATIONSHIP STRESS
Finding/Attracting Love
Direct - *Amethyst, Clear Quartz, Dendritic or Moss Agate, Rose Quartz*
Indirect - *Morganite, Orange Calcite, Rhodonite*
Surrounding - *Angelite, Aquamarine, Black Tourmaline, Selenite*
Suggested Elixir Recipe

RELATIONSHIP STRESS
Healing a Broken Heart
Direct - *Amethyst, Chiastolite, Larimar, Rose Quartz*
Indirect - *Dioptase, Morganite, Orange Calcite, Tangerine Quartz*
Surrounding - *Carnelian, Clear Quartz, Turquoise*
Suggested Elixir Recipe

SPIRITUAL DISCONNECTION

Sometimes life gets us down, and we feel alone. We forget to invite the angels, our guides/guardians and Spirit into our lives to aid, guide or improve our situations. We feel disconnected from everything – especially our faith and spiritual selves. We get so bogged down in the physical, earthly problems that we don't think about asking for Divine help or feel we are not worthy of assistance. We are never alone. Everything has a spirit and is connected to Divine energy, even gemstones. The mineral kingdom is ready to aid us in reestablishing that part of ourselves that is lacking, drained or has forgotten how to "plug in." In some cases, we are in a depression and can't lift ourselves up or energize ourselves. See Chapter 5 for gemstones to use in fighting depression.

Agate – (P)(EM)(EN)(S) Reduces negativity, opens heart to spiritual connection and growth
Amazonite – (EM)(EN)(S) Balances emotions, opens one to higher communication and universal love, clarity in thought *Amber* - (S) Resonates with Archangel Uriel
Ametrine – (P)(EM)(EN)(IN)(S) Raises vibration quickly for meditation and communication, balances emotions and thought patterns, balances body, mind, spirit for clarity, insightfulness, enhances intuition
Amethyst – (P)(EN)(EM)(IN)(S) Harmony in body, mind and spirit, aids in communication, spiritual opening and growth, facilitates positive attitudes and sense of well-being, protection
Angelite (Blue Celestite) – (EN)(S) Opens higher communication and invites angels in for support and aid, promotes peace and harmony amongst all beings, reconnection with universal energy
Apophyllite – (P)(EM)(EN)(IN)(S) Focuses energy, increases strength of connection between physical and spiritual especially in pyramid form, calms mind and emotions, aids in correcting negative behavior patterns, increases link to universal love

Aquamarine – (P)(EM)(EN)(IN)(S) Quiets the intellect or questioning nature of the person to "allow" the process of information to be received, balances emotions and thoughts for better spiritual connection, increases intuition

Auralite 23 – (P)(EM)(EN)(IN)(S) Rebuilds trust in spiritual connections, energizes and motivates, heals past hurts, allows one to see things more clearly, brings larger perspective into focus, makes away of connection to all living things, allows one to calmly deal with past lives and future events

Azeztulite – (P)(EM)(EN)(IN)(S) Connection to higher spiritual self, universal love, guides, guardians, angels, Creator and all earthly beings, raises vibration quickly, opens third eye, calms mind in meditation, heightens intuition and clarity in messages

Azurite –(P)(EM)(EN)(IN)(S) Connection to guides, guardians, angels, Creator and all earthly beings, instill sense of purpose, increases intuitive self, enhances link to universal truth and love

Blue Fluorite – (P)(EM)(EN)(IN)(S) Aids in meditation as it shuts out emotions, worries, mind chatter; raises vibration slowly and holds steady, balances/brings together all bodies (physical, emotional, energetic, intellectual and spiritual in perfect harmony

Citrine – (S) Resonates with Archangel Gabrielle

Danburite – (EN)(S) Heightens vibration for connecting with spiritual realm, aids in enlightenment, soul attunement, eliminates mind chatter, lessens tinnitus

Fulgurite – (EM)(EN)(S) Clearer communication of prayers and answers

Emerald – (S) Resonates with Archangel Raphael

Herkimer Diamond – (P)(EN)(IN)(S) Raises kundalini and mental stimulation for meditation, aids in relaxation, calms mind chatter, boosts confidence in interpreting messages received

Icelandic Spar (Clear Calcite) – (EM)(EN)(IN)(S) Sharpens intuition, clarifies interpretation of visions, removes blockages of third eye and crown chakras, aids in releasing doubts and fears

Infinite – (EM)(EN)(IN)(S) Heals past life injuries, raises consciousness to angelic realms

Iolite – (EN)(IN)(S) Opens third eye, increases spiritual bond, clearer communication and understanding of messages; resonates with Archangel Michael

Jet – (P)(EM)(EN)(IN)(S) Creates a strong Earth to Divine connection, aids in healing, protection

Kunzite – (EM)(EN)(S) Releases doubts, increases trust, restores faith and vision, restores gratitude of life and blessings

Kyanite – (P)(EN)(S) Builds bridges to high self, connect with spirit guides, manifesting spiritual desires

Labradorite – (P)(EM)(EN)(IN)(S) – Calms and reduces stress, quiets thoughts and negativity, opens a doorway to higher spiritual connection, aids in retaining information perceived in meditation

Lapis Lazuli – (S) Resonates with Archangel Michael

Malachite – (S) Resonates with Archangel Raphael

Moldavite – (S) Resonates with Archangel Metatron

Phenacite – (EN)(S) Stimulates third eye, purifies energy, unblocks meridians, enhances communication with angels, guides, higher realms, purifies and harmonizes ethereal and physical bodies, heals and balances chakras

Prehnite – (P)(EM)(EN)(IN)(S) Instills trust in the universe and a higher power, spiritual manifestations

Selenite – (P)(EM)(EN)(IN)(S) Protection, brings negative thoughts to surface to release fear and anger, thoughts and emotions on straighter, positive path, reignites faith and spirituality without religious ties

Seraphinite (Chlorite) – (EM)(EN)(S) Heals holes and spiritual injuries, raises spiritual vibration for clearer communication and reconnection

Shungite – (P)(EN)(EM)(IN)(S) Instill peace, calms nerves and aids in meditation, raising your vibration and spiritual connection while keeping you safely grounded

Sugilite – (S) Resonates with Archangel Michael

Super 7 (Melody Stone) – (P)(EM)(EN)(IN)(S) Reduces distractions allowing for higher consciousness and communication

Tangerine Quartz – (EN)(S) Motivation and clear communication, creativity in spiritual matters, enhances faith and trust in oneself, quiets negative thoughts and patterns

Tektite – (S) Resonates with Archangel Metatron

Yellow Obsidian – (EM)(EN)(IN)(S) Repairs lost faith, increases positive outlook of life and blessings – especially after traumatic events; resonates with Archangel Gabrielle

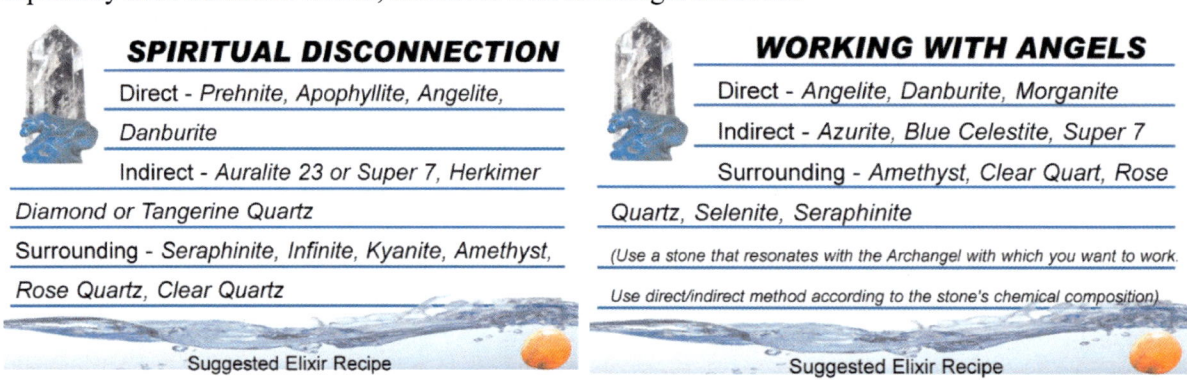

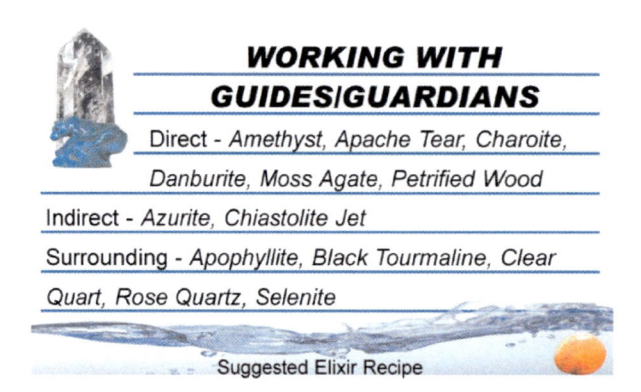

SPIRITUAL DISCONNECTION
Direct - *Prehnite, Apophyllite, Angelite, Danburite*
Indirect - *Auralite 23 or Super 7, Herkimer Diamond or Tangerine Quartz*
Surrounding - *Seraphinite, Infinite, Kyanite, Amethyst, Rose Quartz, Clear Quartz*
Suggested Elixir Recipe

WORKING WITH ANGELS
Direct - *Angelite, Danburite, Morganite*
Indirect - *Azurite, Blue Celestite, Super 7*
Surrounding - *Amethyst, Clear Quart, Rose Quartz, Selenite, Seraphinite*
(Use a stone that resonates with the Archangel with which you want to work. Use direct/indirect method according to the stone's chemical composition)
Suggested Elixir Recipe

WORKING WITH GUIDES/GUARDIANS
Direct - *Amethyst, Apache Tear, Charoite, Danburite, Moss Agate, Petrified Wood*
Indirect - *Azurite, Chiastolite Jet*
Surrounding - *Apophyllite, Black Tourmaline, Clear Quart, Rose Quartz, Selenite*
Suggested Elixir Recipe

CHAPTER FIVE – Emotional Behaviors, Addictions and Bad Habits

"The greatest weapon against stress is our ability to choose one thought over another."
– William James

Everyone has to battle with some type of addiction at one time or another in their lives - food, drugs, alcohol, sex, people, feelings, etc. For some people, it is an ongoing battle throughout their lives. These recipes are to help fight these battles within ourselves. Use them as tools to strengthen resolve, will power and to aid in positive habits and thoughts. Stress, self-image and negativity also come into play. Most addictions stem from emotional trauma and negative patterns. Try to find the emotional trigger in your addiction and use stones that will aid you in repairing the emotional as well as the physical damage.

(Remember to balance your chakras, so that your energy is more in balance to aid in your fight and lifestyle changes.)

QUIT SMOKING/TOBACCO ADDICTION
Amethyst – Helps break addictions, detoxifies, heals disease, clears/strengthens lungs, respiratory system
Ametrine – Same properties as Amethyst and Citrine, strengthens resolve and reinforces the wish to change/break habits
Apache Tear – Release of bad habits/breaking patterns, calms nerves, removes toxins
Aquamarine – Aids in breaking the addiction, cleanses throat and lungs, encourages healthier lifestyle
Auralite 23 – Rebuilds good habits and patterns, cleanses, heals on cellular level, instills can-do attitude
Azeztulite – Helps body reject unhealthy habits, substances, detoxifies, regenerates healthy cells/tissues
Azurite – Detoxification, realigns thought patterns for success, balances chakras, transmutes fear, aids transformation
Barite – Cleanses and rebalances chakras, supports memory, boosts vitality, detoxifies, fights addiction and depression
Black Tourmaline – Rebuilds metabolism and reconnection to organic/healthy eating and lifestyle, instills positive attitude
Blue Chalcedony (Agate) - Heals the lungs and clears the respiratory system of effects of smoke/smoking
Botswana Agate – Aids in breaking up the routine, cleanses circulatory and respiratory systems, fights depression and smoking
Brown Jasper - Eases nicotine cravings, cleanses mouth, throat, taste buds, strengthens willpower and elimination system
Charoite – Reduces nicotine cravings, heightens resolve, increases positive mood/outlook, transforms disease into health
Chiastolite – Breaks old habits, increases resolve, invites spiritual strength and support, eases nervousness
Citrine - Helps with transitioning, releases stress and fear, cleanses and detoxifies physically as well as energetically
Diopside – Clears lungs, strengthens respiratory and circulatory tract, healing of heart muscle, recovery, breaks addictions
Fulgurite – Prayers and resolve to quit strengthened, easier breathing, transformation reinforced, breaks blockages

Green Calcite – Breaks habits, relieves cravings and pain, reinforces good habits and patterns, strengthens respiratory tract, immune system and heart

Green Jasper – Heals and strengthens lungs, creates nausea if smokes, breaks obsessions, reduces toxins

Hematite – Reduces nicotine cravings, strengthens resolve, builds up energy, aids circulatory system

Iolite – Pinpoints causes of addiction and aids in releasing toxins – emotionally, physically and mentally, lessens codependency,

Jade- Removes toxins, strengthens adrenals and elimination system, increases energy and channels it constructively

Kunzite/Hiddenite – Joy/gratitude and higher spiritual strength for continued success in quitting, benefits lungs and chest

Kyanite – Builds better habits and strengthens desire to quit, creative solutions to cravings, aids throat and adrenals

Labradorite –Calms anger, reduces stress, detoxifies, instills optimism and hope, helps lungs and respiratory system

Malachite – Increases willpower and self-confidence, cleanses body of toxins, cellular regeneration

Moldavite – Aids in life transformations, breaks down old/builds up new, healing on all levels, energizes

Peridot – Healing at cellular level, strengthens lungs, heart, respiratory tract, vocal chords, metabolism

Rose Quartz – Self love, self confidence, brings energy bodies into harmony to strengthen determination

Shungite - Detoxifies, purifies and cleanses your body of harmful chemicals, bacteria and heavy metals, aids one in cutting the dependency and cravings, strengthens resolve to quit

Sunstone – Instills a take charge attitude and faith in oneself, nurturing, renews joy of life, battles procrastination

Tektite - Aids in life transformations, breaks down old/builds up new, energizes and encourages physical activity

Tiger Eye – Balance, strengthens willpower, builds confidence, dissolves blockages, aids throat

Turquoise – Encourages wholeness in physical health and emotions, dispels self-destructive habits, assimilation of vitamins and minerals, anti-inflammatory and detoxifies.

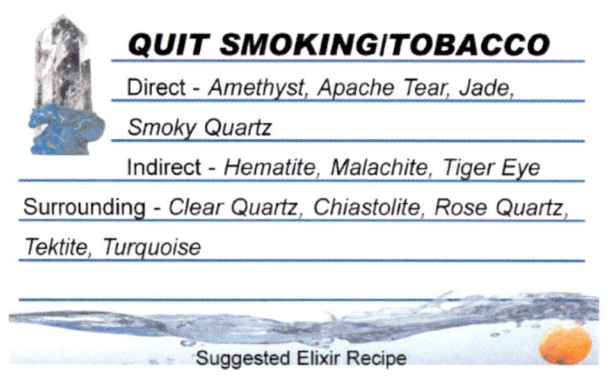

QUIT SMOKING/TOBACCO

Direct - *Amethyst, Apache Tear, Jade, Smoky Quartz*

Indirect - *Hematite, Malachite, Tiger Eye*

Surrounding - *Clear Quartz, Chiastolite, Rose Quartz, Tektite, Turquoise*

Suggested Elixir Recipe

ALCOHOL & DRUG ADDICTION

Amethyst – Break addictions, detoxifies, heals disease, balances emotional, physical and mental bodies

Ametrine - Same properties as amethyst; strengthens resolve, reinforces the will to change/break habits

Apatite – Instills will-power and aids in achieving goals, dissolves negativity

Aquamarine – Release of emotions in a healthy and safe way, instills a feeling of peace and safety, reduces stress, detoxifies, reduces cravings for alcohol

Aragonite – Teaches patience, positive outlook, re-instills faith in oneself, calms nerves

Auralite 23 – Rebuilds good habits and patterns, cleanses, heals on cellular level, instills can-do attitude

Azurite – Detoxification, realigns thought patterns for success, balances chakras, transmutes fear, aids transformation, heals gallbladder, kidney and liver

Barite - Aids in freedom of addictions, releases bad habits, fears and old emotional patterns, detoxification, rebalances chakras, supports memory, boosts vitality

Carnelian – Detoxification, harmony of all energy bodies, combats depression, strengthens resolve, speeds up healing process

Charoite – Transmutes negativity, treats liver and elimination systems, reenergizes and detoxifies, heals liver after alcohol abuse, instills a sense of duty to help one-self and others as well as will to live a wholesome life

Fire Agate – Heals stomach, liver, instills sense of security, aids in introspection, eliminates cravings, breaks bad habits

Fluorite – Works at cellular level heals and regenerates cells, calms nerves, releases emotional trauma /destructive habits

Green Jasper – Eliminates bloating, decreases cravings, cleanses and strengthens liver and digestive tract

Green Tourmaline – Patience, compassion, balance, rejuvenation, detoxifies, calms nerves and fears, enhances positive growth

Hematite- Aids circulatory and elimination systems, removes self limitations and destructive thoughts, enhances willpower to overcome addictions and compulsions

Iolite – Pinpoints causes of addiction and aids in releasing toxins – emotionally, physically and mentally, lessens codependency, increases immune system and regenerates liver

Jade – Cleanses and strengthens immune, elimination and circulatory systems, release of negative thoughts, balances fluids and acid/alkaline ratios

Kyanite – Builds better habits and strengthens desire to quit, creative solutions to cravings, aids throat and adrenals

Kunzite/Hiddenite – Combats depression and self destructive habits, physical and emotional harmony, encourages self confidence, willpower and new beginnings

Labradorite –Reduces stress, detoxifies, instills optimism and hope, aids digestive system and organs

Moss Agate – Replaces negativity with positive, allows one to see their inner beauty and goodness, detoxification

Obsidian (Apache Tear) – Cleanses and detoxifies, strengthens will power and good self-image, aids in transformation and establishing good habits

Orange Calcite – Settles stomach and gastrointestinal issues, soothes emotions and heals ulcers, enhance calcium absorption, encourages pain management and less toxic drug use

Ruby – Detoxifies and boosts immune, circulation, elimination and respiratory systems, liver and spleen

Serpentine – Balances body sugars, balances mentally and emotionally, aids in establishing new paths and habits, self control

Shungite - Detoxifies, purifies and cleanses your body of harmful chemicals, bacteria and heavy metals, aids one in cutting the dependency and cravings, strengthens resolve to quit

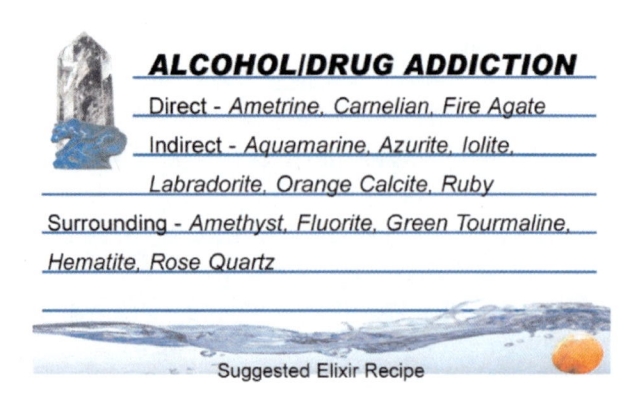

ALCOHOL/DRUG ADDICTION
Direct - *Ametrine, Carnelian, Fire Agate*
Indirect - *Aquamarine, Azurite, Iolite, Labradorite, Orange Calcite, Ruby*
Surrounding - *Amethyst, Fluorite, Green Tourmaline, Hematite, Rose Quartz*

Suggested Elixir Recipe

FOOD ADDICTION/ WEIGHT ISSUES

Amazonite – Benefits metabolism, nutrition and calcium absorption, alleviates stress, promotes self image

Amethyst – Overall health, de-stressor, detoxifies, blocks cravings, balances metabolism and emotions, encourages good habits

Apatite (Yellow in particular) – Decreases cravings and hunger, encourages healthy eating, raises metabolism, aids digestion and elimination, balances physical, mental, emotional and energetic bodies, instills will-power and aids in achieving goals,

Aventurine – Balances cholesterol, aids thyroid, stimulates metabolism, benefits heart and circulation

Auralite 23 – Rebuilds good habits/patterns, cleanses and heals on cellular level, instills can-do attitude

Azeztulite – Will power, positive attitude, aids cancer and bulimia patients with weight gain, stimulates appetite, will to live and sense of purpose

Azurite – Successful goal setting and attainment, aids transformation and being best self at any weight, self-confidence

Bloodstone – Stimulates metabolism, immune system and aids circulatory system, detoxifies and eliminates, increases water consumption, reenergizes

Botswana Agate – Lessens reaction to food allergies, removes toxins, balances weight

Carnelian – Cleanses, detoxifies, harmonizes digestive, elimination and circulatory systems, balances enzymes, eliminates parasites, raises metabolism

Clear Quartz - Energizes and encourages exercising, purifies, detoxifies digestive system, aids adrenals

Danburite – Raises vibration and mood, spiritual support, detoxifies, lowers cholesterol, aids gallbladder

Fire Agate – Instills willpower and positive change attitude, boosts energy, removes blockages and cleanses elimination system

Fluorite – Fights binge eating and stress, purifies and cleanses, aids metabolism, promotes overall good health and habits

Green Tourmaline – Encourages weight loss, healthy metabolism, absorption of nutrients, healthier diet, good for thyroid, thymus and immune system

Hemimorphite – Aids in self-transformation, self-image, support for dieting and maintaining health

Iolite – Breaks down fatty deposits, removes toxins, raises spirit and vibrational energy as well as physical energy

Lapis Lazuli – Releases pain and negative thoughts/habits, enhances motivation, goal-setting and achievement, sustain health, support thyroid, thymus and immune system

Kyanite – Aids diet by combating excessive weight, raises awareness of eating habits and nutrient absorption, balances thyroid

Labradorite – Calms anger, reduces stress, instills optimism and hope, aids digestive system/metabolism

Magnesite – Motivation, stimulation, energy, balancing metabolism

Mica (Fuchsite/Muscovite) - Stimulates thyroid, kidneys, cleansing system, makes you feel "full" after eating smaller amounts, aids in nutrient absorption and digestion, balances blood sugar levels

Moss Agate – Aids digestion, willpower, self image, water consumption, goal attainment and balance

Peridot – Aids in recognition of bad eating habits and modifying them, decreases cravings, stimulates elimination system and treats ulcers and stomach abnormalities

Petrified Wood – Stone of new beginnings and transformation, strengthens will power and resolutions for good eating habits

Red Jasper – Encourages healthy eating, cleanses and detoxifies digestive system, increases energy and promotes healthy habits and exercise, encourages positive emotions and self-image

Rose Quartz – Unconditional acceptance of oneself (physically, emotionally, spiritually), balance/harmony of bodies, stops binging/purging, overeating tendencies, detoxifies, de-stresses

Serpentine – Aids in shedding of the old and transformation of the new, decreases appetite, balances sugar levels, absorption of calcium and magnesium, strengthens digestive and elimination systems

Sulfur – Eliminates bad habits, discourages overeating, encourages positive self-image, aids in "melting" away fat

Sunstone – Instills take charge attitude, faith in self, nurturing, renews joy of life, battles procrastination

Turquoise – Helps envision a healthier self, a positive self-image, breaks things down into easier steps, living in the now and reaffirming goals, strengthens body, mind and spirit, aids in absorption of nutrients

Unakite – Strengthens goals, aids in achievement, promotes healthier lifestyle, aids in repairing existing physical and emotional damage, rebuilds positive self-image

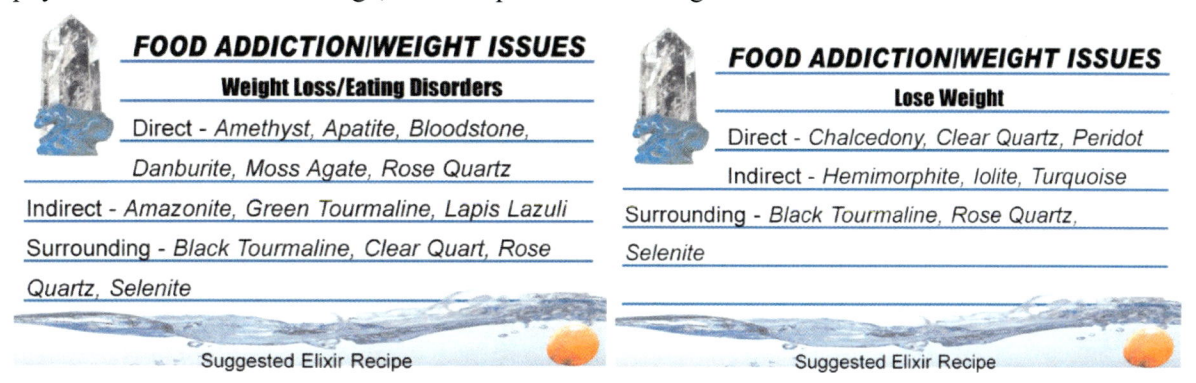

FOOD ADDICTION/WEIGHT ISSUES
Weight Loss/Eating Disorders

Direct - *Amethyst, Apatite, Bloodstone, Danburite, Moss Agate, Rose Quartz*

Indirect - *Amazonite, Green Tourmaline, Lapis Lazuli*

Surrounding - *Black Tourmaline, Clear Quart, Rose Quartz, Selenite*

Suggested Elixir Recipe

FOOD ADDICTION/WEIGHT ISSUES
Lose Weight

Direct - *Chalcedony, Clear Quartz, Peridot*

Indirect - *Hemimorphite, Iolite, Turquoise*

Surrounding - *Black Tourmaline, Rose Quartz, Selenite*

Suggested Elixir Recipe

FOOD ADDICTION/WEIGHT ISSUES
Gain Weight
Direct - *Azeztulite, Danburite, Peridot, Unakite*
Indirect - *Fluorite, Turquoise*
Surrounding - *Black Tourmaline, Clear Quart, Rose Quartz, Selenite*

Suggested Elixir Recipe

FOOD ADDICTION/WEIGHT ISSUES
Bulimia
Direct - *Phenacite, Danburite, Rose Quartz*
Indirect - *Fluorite, Morganite, Sulfur*
Surrounding - *Black Tourmaline, Clear Quart, Rose Quartz, Selenite*

Suggested Elixir Recipe

DEPRESSION/MENTAL ANXIETY/FEARS

Agate - (Moss) Heals emotional disease (Pink) Balances left/right brain, Botswana – depression and stress
Amber - Promotes positive mental state and patience, clears depression, balances emotions, memory aid
Amethyst - Balances highs and lows; dispels rage, fear, sadness and grief, balances body, mind and spirit
Ametrine - Heals depression, strengthens concentration
Apache Tear (Obsidian) – Strengthens character, reduces stress, removes negativity and toxicity of thoughts, actions and words
Apatite- (Yellow) Treats depression and lethargy, energizes
Apophyllite - Relieves stress, releases negative thought patterns, feeling of being connected to all things
Auralite 23 – Calms nerves, relaxes anxiety, releases anger and emotions safely and constructively
Barite - Enhances love, releases and calms emotions, reduces fear and harmony in relationship
Blue Lace Agate - Calms nerves and butterflies in the stomach, aids digestion
Botswana Agate – Fights depression and stress, creates more positive thought patterns
Calcite (Gold/Honey) - Relieves depression, mood uplifter
Calcite (Orange) – Aids in overcoming depression, balances emotions, removes fear, dissolves problems, uplifts emotions, restores childlike wonder and curiosity
Carnelian - Protection from own and others rage/anger, banishes negative emotions
Charoite – Aids in healing bipolar disorders, decreases anxiety, frustration and obsession
Chiastolite - Dispels negative thoughts and feelings, encourages healthy connections wit Spirit
Citrine - Aids in overcoming depression, fears and phobias
Clear Quartz – Restores and enhances energy physically, mentally, emotionally
Danburite – Uplifts and transcends negativity, reinforces connection to spirit and a positive outlook
Iolite - Dispels depression and aids in refocusing on the positive and finding right path for individual
Jet - Keeps one safe from outside influences, rebuilds confidence, restores faith in self and taking control/responsibility for one's own life
Kyanite – Bring peace of mind, compassion, boost decision making and logical thoughts, aids with communication and organization, release of fears and negativity
Kunzite (& Hiddenite) - Lithium based - treats psychiatric disorders and depression, allows self to see blessings and restores gratitude and joy
Labradorite – Calms anger, reduces stress, instills optimism, patience and hope, allow better decisions by seeing larger picture

Lapis Lazuli - Overcomes depression, releases endorphins, relieves pain
Lepidolite- Releases stress, battles depression, aids acceptance of change, soothes nerves, fights insomnia
Lithium - Antidepressant, neutralizes anger and grief, energy amplifier
Morganite - Encourages positive view, works as a sedative, cleanses mentality, opens heart for unconditional love and healing
Peridot - Balances bipolar disorder, aids in healing brain electricity blockages and misfires
Sardonyx - Alleviates depression and overcomes hesitancy
Serpentine – Raises emotions and mental state, stimulates crown and heart chakras, directs emotional, mental, intellectual and spiritual healing energies where needed
Sunstone – Combats depression and re-energizes, raises vibration for a "take charge" attitude
Tangerine Quartz – Enhances faith and trust in oneself, quiets negative thoughts, removal of negative behaviors
Tiger Eye - Battles mental disease and personality disorders, rebalances emotions and body/mind
Tourmaline - Mental balance *(Green & Black)* Encourages positive attitude; *(Watermelon)* Alleviates depression and fear
Turquoise - Relieves exhaustion, depression and panic attacks, encourages one to put pieces back together
Yellow Obsidian – Mental stimulation and mood uplifter, calms nerves, de-stressor

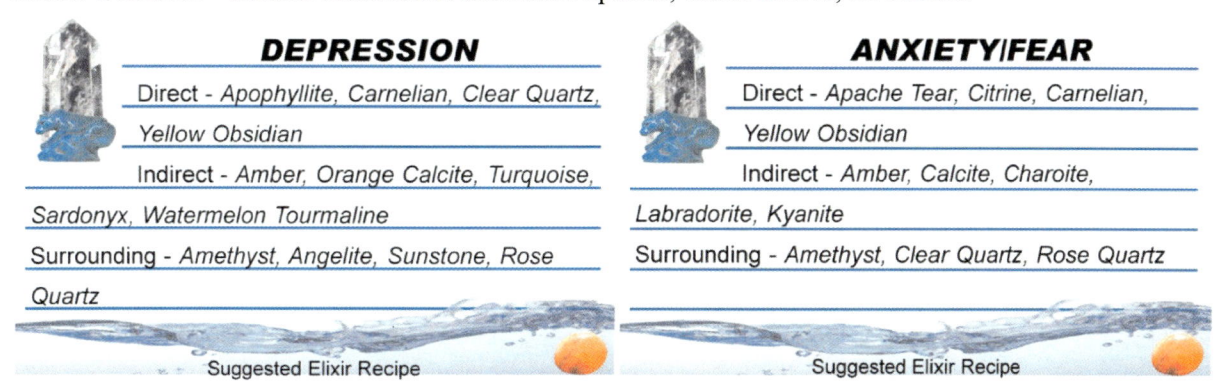

DEPRESSION

Direct - *Apophyllite, Carnelian, Clear Quartz, Yellow Obsidian*

Indirect - *Amber, Orange Calcite, Turquoise, Sardonyx, Watermelon Tourmaline*

Surrounding - *Amethyst, Angelite, Sunstone, Rose Quartz*

Suggested Elixir Recipe

ANXIETY/FEAR

Direct - *Apache Tear, Citrine, Carnelian, Yellow Obsidian*

Indirect - *Amber, Calcite, Charoite, Labradorite, Kyanite*

Surrounding - *Amethyst, Clear Quartz, Rose Quartz*

Suggested Elixir Recipe

ANGER/GRIEF/EMOTIONAL TURMOIL
(Also see Relationship Stress in Chapter Four)
Agate – Balances emotional, physical and intellectual bodies, reduces anger and tension
Amazonite – Releases feelings of anger, worry and fear, brings emotions into balance
Amethyst – Balances feelings – equalizes highs and lows so you don't lose your temper
Angelite/Blue Celestite – Promotes harmony, relieves feelings of anger, fear and stress
Apache Tear – Release of grief and negative emotions, past traumas, nightmares
Aquamarine – Release of emotions in a healthy and safe way, instills tolerance, peace and safety, promotes healing in the grieving process, acceptance
Aragonite – Dispels anger, combats stress, acceptance of what can't change, brings insight.perspective
Auralite 23 – Calms nerves, relaxes anxiety, releases anger and emotions safely and constructively
Aventurine – Protects heart and emotions, allows grieving and moving forward, calms mind and emotions
Blue Lace Agate – Calms anger, brings up feelings and allows for expression without judgment or anger
Carnelian – Calms anger, grief, envy, resentment, balances emotions, promotes love and acceptance

Chiastolite – Changes conflict into harmony, dispel negative thoughts and feelings, calms fears, brings comfort to grief-stricken or transitioning souls and their loved ones, releases feelings of guilt

Chrysoprase – Calms anger and helps hold back harmful words, balances emotions, acceptance of own and others limitation

Dioptase – Relieves grief/sorrow, forgiveness of self and others, cools temper

Labradorite – Calms anger, reduces stress, supports intelligent decisions, instills optimism and hope

Magnetite – Helps to work through guilt and grief, feelings of anger and fear, instills feeling of safety, emotional balance

Malachite – Personal will, standing up for self in positive, non-aggressive way

Moonstone – Personal strength and empowerment, calms fears and anger

Morganite – Calms stress, opens heart and mind, heals soul, higher perspective

Obsidian (Black/Rainbow/Apache Tear) – Releases fear, calms emotions after bringing the cause to the surface for examination and release, protection from negativity

Orange Calcite – Mood uplifter, peaceful feelings toward others

Rhodonite – Balances emotions, encourages love, heals emotional trauma and aids with forgiveness, defeats self-destruction

Rose Quartz – Unconditional love for self and others, empathy, cools temper

Sugilite – Releases sorrow and feelings of guilt, removes hostility and fear

Tangerine Quartz – (EM) (EN) Releases negative emotions, restores balance in feelings, promotes optimism and better outlook

Turitella Agate – (P) (EM) Aids/supports transitions, reduces stress, acceptance, calms stomach

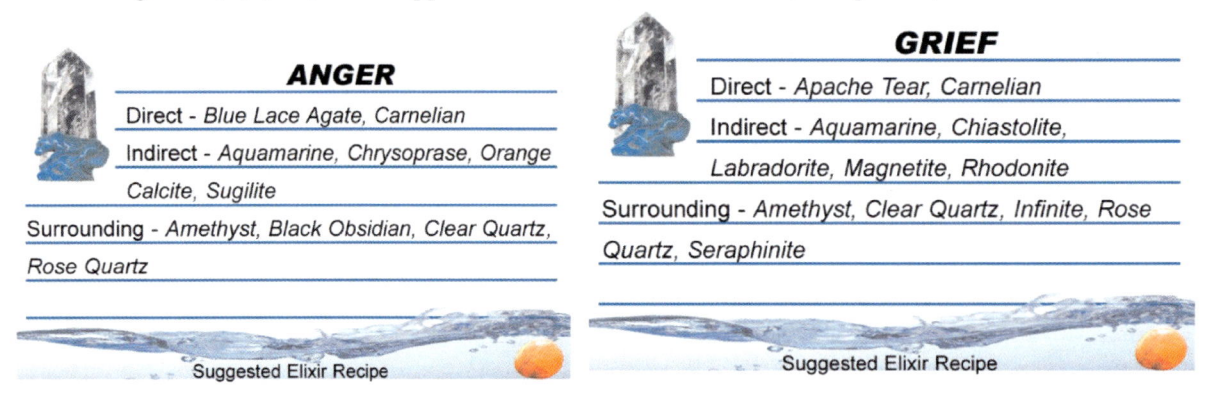

ANGER
Direct - *Blue Lace Agate, Carnelian*
Indirect - *Aquamarine, Chrysoprase, Orange Calcite, Sugilite*
Surrounding - *Amethyst, Black Obsidian, Clear Quartz, Rose Quartz*

Suggested Elixir Recipe

GRIEF
Direct - *Apache Tear, Carnelian*
Indirect - *Aquamarine, Chiastolite, Labradorite, Magnetite, Rhodonite*
Surrounding - *Amethyst, Clear Quartz, Infinite, Rose Quartz, Seraphinite*

Suggested Elixir Recipe

CHAPTER SIX - Immune Building, Colds/Flu/Respiratory

Gemstones work with us by speeding up things that would happen naturally in our bodies or energy field. For instance, working with a carnelian for the common cold, symptoms will appear to get worse as our bodies speed up the process of ridding us of the virus. Instead of a long drawn out cold, your body heals itself on a quicker scale. This can also work for our emotional, mental and spiritual issues. A good first-aid kit for any condition would be the combination of Clear Quartz, Rose Quartz and Amethyst. These three gemstones combined will purify, detoxify, boost energy and bring healing to your body, mind and spirit. Depending on your symptoms, you may want to combine immune, cold and respiratory gemstones for a stronger elixir that will fight the disease and alleviate your symptoms while strengthening your body. (When you see a color in a parenthesis after a stone, it means the whole family of these stones work on this condition, but the color specified is stronger than the others.)

GENERAL HEALTH
(Multivitamin/Mineral – Strengthen Immune System)

Amber – Antifungal, Antibacterial, balances body, mind, spirit and energy fields, treats throat, kidneys, bladder and urinary tract infections/illnesses

Amethyst – Overall healer, calms nerves, balances hormones, strengthens endocrine, elimination, respiratory, metabolism and immune systems; works on cellular disorders

Apatite – Works with calcium to strengthen bones and teeth, aids overall function of cells, aids elimination and digestive systems

Auralite23 - Balances emotions, reduces pain, promotes healing of muscles, nerves, tissues as well as elimination system, healing and restructuring on a cellular level, calms and soothes emotions and tension of body, encourages one to "just breathe" live in the moment

Calcite – Assists metabolism and nutrient absorption, aids bones and joints

Green Calcite – Cleansing, inspires growth, dissolves calcifications, creates emotional intelligence, tissue healing, elimination, skin and skeletal systems

Carnelian – Vitality, metabolism, arthritis, joints, bones, ligaments, absorption of nutrients

Clear Quartz – Energy, purification/detoxification, focused healing

Copper – Stimulates metabolism, assists in absorption of nutrients and iron, strengthens and purifies circulatory system, aids building healthy red blood cells and prevention of disease, blocks free radicals

Galena – Beneficial to hair, skin, nails and circulatory system, reduces inflammation, stimulates absorption of zinc and selenium

Hematite – Aids circulatory and digestive systems, reduces anxiety, reduces pain in muscles and joints

Herkimer Diamond – Relieves spot pain quickly, boosts metabolism, mood lifter, increases energy

Indicolite – Helps diagnose health issues, brings hidden feelings and stressors to surface for healing, combats insomnia, aids circulatory, pulmonary, respiratory and elimination systems, treats eyes, ears, nose, throat issues, kidneys, bladder

Infinite – Pain relief for muscles and cramps, balances sugar, strengthens pancreas, combined with Seraphinite is overall healer and rejuvenator

Jade – Cleansing, elimination system, spleen, alkaline balance

Labradorite – Reduces stress, aids digestive system and metabolism, strengthens respiratory and circulatory systems, reduces pain

Larimar – Nurtures body and spirit, energy booster for new mothers, absorption of nutrients

Mica (Fuchsite/Muscovite) – Balances pH and potassium levels, detoxifies blood, aids kidneys in eliminating poisons

Orange Calcite – Settles stomach and gastrointestinal issues, soothes emotions and heals ulcers, enhance calcium absorption, encourages pain management and less toxic drug use

Peridot – Purifies physically, mentally and emotionally, reduces stress and motivates positive changes, strengthens thymus, glands, gallbladder, kidneys, lungs, eyes

Pietersite – Relieves exhaustion in those who don't take time to rest, stimulates thymus, thyroid and pituitary glands

Rose Quartz – Unconditional love, emotions, strengthens heart, elimination and circulatory system,

Selenite – Creates a peaceful environment, protection, aligns spine and promotes flexibility, guards against epileptic seizures, reverses effects of free radicals

Septarian – Focuses healing where needed, boosts metabolism, aids digestive and elimination systems

Seraphinite – Releases toxins, aids absorption of vitamins and minerals, pain relief, acidophilus like properties

Shungite- Anti-bacterial, anti-inflammatory, strengthens all body systems, detoxifies and cleanses blood

Sulfur – External use only, enhances hair, nails and skin, oxygenation of red blood cells, detoxifier, assists with enzymes

Super 7 – Raises emotions and combats depression, reduces pain, aids circulatory and digestive systems, healing and restructuring on a cellular level

Turitella Agate – Aids/supports transitions, reduces stress, assimilation of calcium, vitamins and minerals

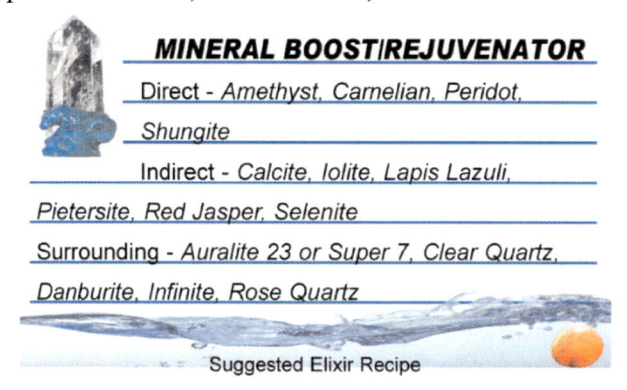

MINERAL BOOST/REJUVENATOR
Direct - *Amethyst, Carnelian, Peridot, Shungite*
Indirect - *Calcite, Iolite, Lapis Lazuli, Pietersite, Red Jasper, Selenite*
Surrounding - *Auralite 23 or Super 7, Clear Quartz, Danburite, Infinite, Rose Quartz*
Suggested Elixir Recipe

STRENGTHEN/BOOST IMMUNE SYSTEM

Amethyst - Strengthens immune, respiratory and elimination systems, boosts metabolism

Ametrine - Strengthens immune system and regenerates the physical body

Aquamarine - Assimilation of vitamins and minerals, cleanses and eliminates toxins

Aragonite - Boosts immune and circulatory systems

Bloodstone - Energy cleanser, immune stimulator, detoxifier

Calcite - Fortifies immune system, cleanses elimination organs, strengthens bones and joints

Carnelian - Cleanses digestive and elimination systems, brings physical body into harmony, energizes and revitalizes, stimulates appetite and absorption of vitamins and minerals
Clear Quartz – Strengthens, cleanses and energizes total body
Copper – Boosts, fortifies and purifies circulatory and immune system, combats bacteria infections
Emerald – Strength, recovery and regeneration
Halite (salt) – Cleanses, detoxifies and purifies the lungs and environment
Hematite – Strengthens circulatory system, cleanses on cellular level
Iolite - Aids sinuses and respiratory tract, boosts immune system
Jade – Strengthens elimination system/kidneys, detoxifies, de-stress, balances alkalinity and body fluids
Kyanite - Combats infections and rebuilds immune system
Labradorite – Reduces stress, aids digestive system, respiratory and circulatory systems, reduces pain
Magnetite/Lodestone – Boosts compromised immune system to aid in recovery, re-energizes, balances electrolytes
Malachite – Detoxifies, reduces pain, lowers blood pressure, boosts immune system, protects of organs
Moss Agate - Boosts immune system, cleanses circulatory and elimination systems
Peridot – Strengthens and balances whole body and mind
Sardonyx – Regulate metabolism, body fluids, alkalinity, nutrient absorption, strengthens immune system
Septarian – Focuses healing where needed, boosts metabolism, aids digestive and elimination systems
Shungite- Anti-bacterial, anti-inflammatory, strengthens all body systems, detoxifies and cleanses blood
Sodalite - Boosts immune system, promotes healthy sleeping habits, balances body fluids, lowers blood pressure
Sunstone – Aids body in taking control and eliminating disease, stimulates and boosts immune system
Super 7 – Aids the body in healing itself, balances chakras, brings feeling of peace
Zincite – Boosts energy and immune system, works against auto-immune diseases, strengthens elimination system

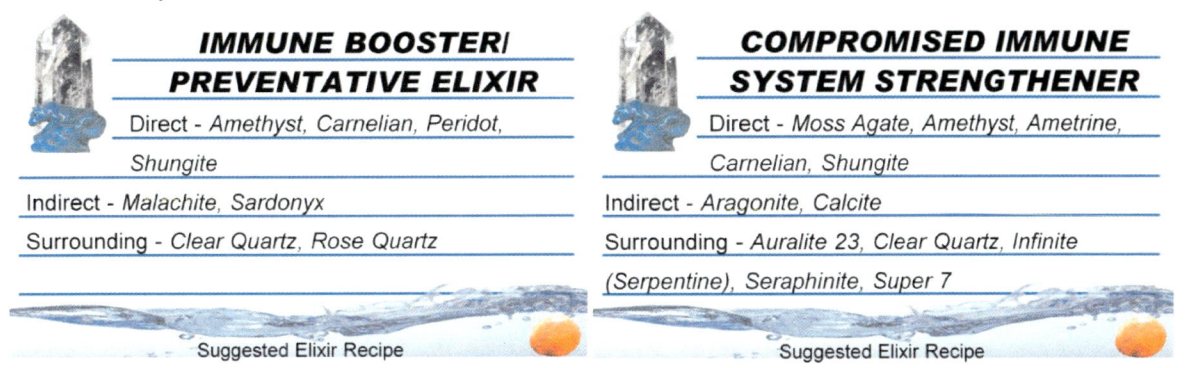

IMMUNE BOOSTER/ PREVENTATIVE ELIXIR	**COMPROMISED IMMUNE SYSTEM STRENGTHENER**
Direct - *Amethyst, Carnelian, Peridot, Shungite*	Direct - *Moss Agate, Amethyst, Ametrine, Carnelian, Shungite*
Indirect - *Malachite, Sardonyx*	Indirect - *Aragonite, Calcite*
Surrounding - *Clear Quartz, Rose Quartz*	Surrounding - *Auralite 23, Clear Quartz, Infinite (Serpentine), Seraphinite, Super 7*
Suggested Elixir Recipe	Suggested Elixir Recipe

COLD/FLU/FEVERS
Agate - Antibacterial, settles stomach/nausea, reduces fever
Amber – Antibacterial and antifungal, purifies air, skin, elixir works like penicillin
Amethyst – Strengthens immune, respiratory and elimination systems, boosts metabolism, lessens symptoms and pain
Angelite – Fights infections, inflammation and fever

Aquamarine – Treats swollen glands, inflammation of the throat
Aragonite – Reduces fever, eliminates chills, cold hands and feet
Blue Lace Agate - Neutralizes fevers and infections, relieves sore throats, cleanses lungs
Moss Agate - Speeds up recovery, boosts immune system, treats colds, flu and infections, lowers fevers
Carnelian – Speeds up recovery, boosts metabolism, immune system and elimination system, nutrient absorption, energizes
Fluorite - Aids in treatment of viruses, infections, colds, flu, sinusitis, bronchitis, clears mucus, pain relief
Emerald – Strength, detoxification, aids recovery and boost energy
Hematite - Helps to reduce fevers, cleanses circulatory system, boosts absorption of iron
Indicolite (Blue Tourmaline) - Helps treat lungs, sinusitis, relieves congestion, reduces fever/sore throat
Iolite - Treats fevers, malaria, kills bacteria, aids sinuses and respiratory tract, boosts immune system
Jet - Good for treating colds and nausea, fights against further infection or progression of disease
Kyanite - Reduces fevers and relieves pain, balances blood pressure, aids throat, lungs and brain
Labradorite - Fights colds, helps with nutrient absorption and balancing metabolism, treats bronchitis and lung conditions, reduces pain and fever
Moss Agate – Detoxifies, combats colds and flu, infections and viruses
Red/black Obsidian - Takes care of fevers and chills, boosts vitamin and mineral absorption, detoxifies, reduces pain
Opal - Reduces fevers and treats infections; green opal alleviates colds and flu
Ruby - Treats fevers and infectious diseases, re-energizes, detoxifies
Sardonyx - Heals lungs, reduces mucus, decongests
Strawberry Quartz – Reduces mucous, expectorant/decongestant
Sulfur - Helps to reduce fevers and infections, relieves pain

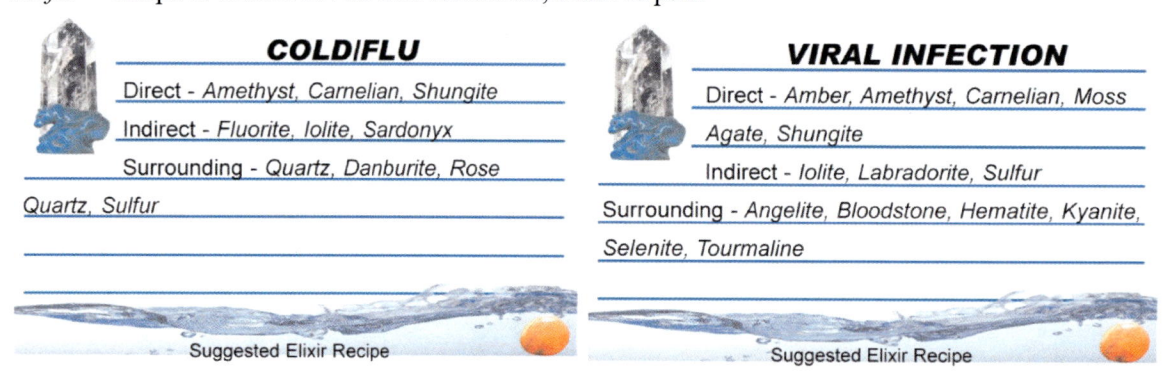

COLD/FLU
Direct - *Amethyst, Carnelian, Shungite*
Indirect - *Fluorite, Iolite, Sardonyx*
Surrounding - *Quartz, Danburite, Rose Quartz, Sulfur*

Suggested Elixir Recipe

VIRAL INFECTION
Direct - *Amber, Amethyst, Carnelian, Moss Agate, Shungite*
Indirect - *Iolite, Labradorite, Sulfur*
Surrounding - *Angelite, Bloodstone, Hematite, Kyanite, Selenite, Tourmaline*

Suggested Elixir Recipe

SORE THROAT/INFECTIONS/DISORDERS
Amber – Treats sore throats, infections, goiters and other throat problems, antibacterial and antifungal
Amethyst – Disinfects, reduces pain, calms nerves
Angelite - Alleviates throat inflammation and irritation, fights infections
Aquamarine - Good for sore throats, swollen glands and thyroid problems
Atacamite - Heals the thyroid gland, opens throat chakra and removes blockages
Azurite - Treats sore throat problems, tonsillitis
Bloodstone - Immune stimulator for acute infections

Blue Lace Agate - Cools, soothes and heals throat infections, thyroid deficiencies, releases neck tension
Chrysocolla - Aids in treating throat infections and tonsillitis, mucus and increases ease of breathing
Fluorite (Blue) - Treats throat problems and conditions - strep, sore throat, inflammation, infections
Garnet - Soothes sore throat and encourages healing
Indicolite (Blue Tourmaline) - Treats chronic sore throat and infections
Kyanite - Treats thyroid, parathyroid, adrenal glands and throat problems
Lapis Lazuli - Alleviates pain and beneficial for throat, larynx and thyroid
Larimar - Beneficial healing for throat problems
Shungite- Anti-bacterial, anti-inflammatory, strengthens all body systems, detoxifies and cleanses blood
Sunstone - Treats chronic sore throats
Tiger Eye - Heals throat and dissolves constrictions

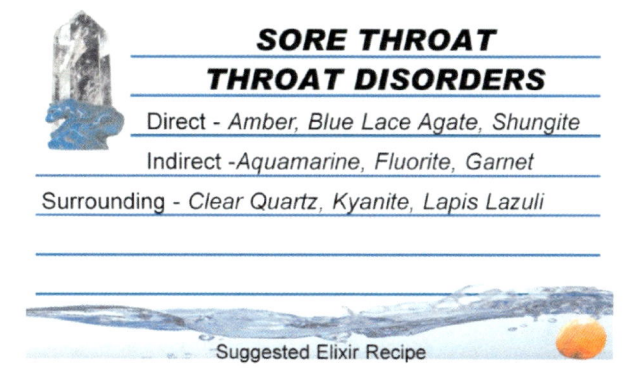

SORE THROAT THROAT DISORDERS
Direct - *Amber, Blue Lace Agate, Shungite*
Indirect - *Aquamarine, Fluorite, Garnet*
Surrounding - *Clear Quartz, Kyanite, Lapis Lazuli*

Suggested Elixir Recipe

ASTHMA/LUNG & RESPIRATORY PROBLEMS

Salt lamps are a great way of cleansing the air and your lungs, whether they are plugged in or not. Salt mine workers are said to be healthier and less susceptible to disease and respiratory problems than the average person.

Amethyst - Heals lungs and respiratory disease, treats body, mind, spirit, detoxifies, eases asthma attacks, combats allergies
Angelite - Stimulates healing of the lungs, calms coughs and irritation of bronchial passage
Aquamarine – Calms allergies and cough, treats hay fever
Apophyllite - Works on respiratory and circulatory system, eases asthma attacks and allergies
Aventurine - Heals lungs, sinuses and respiratory system, reduces coughing, expectorant
Blue Chalcedony (Agate) – Reduces inflammation of and cleanses the respiratory, lymphatic and circulatory systems
Chrysocolla - Combats lung problems, reduces mucus and increases ease of breathing, treats throat infections, balances metabolism, fights infections
Emerald - Treats sinuses and lungs, detoxifies, relieves coughing spasms
Garnet - Purifies and reenergizes lungs, nutrient absorption
Halite (salt) – Cleanses, detoxifies and purifies the lungs and environment
Indicolite (Blue Tourmaline) - Treats lungs and sinusitis, relieves congestion, reduces fever/sore throat
Iolite - Aids the sinuses and strengthens respiratory system, relieves symptoms
Iron Pyrite - Alleviates asthma and bronchitis, benefits the lungs

Labradorite - Fights colds and flu, treats bronchitis and lung conditions, reduces pain and fever

Lapis Lazuli - Benefits the respiratory system, cleanses the lungs, pain relief and decongests

Magnetite - Treats asthma, provides healing energy for recuperation, detoxifies, relieves coughing

Malachite - Aids in treatment of asthma

Morganite - Oxygenates cells, treats emphysema, asthma, lung blockages, tuberculosis, reduces bronchial irritation

Petalite - Aids lungs, regenerates lung tissue, decongests, relieves coughing spasms

Pink Tourmaline - Heals lungs, detoxifies and cleanses bronchial system

Rhodochrosite - Relieves asthma and respiratory problems, cleanses and strengthens lungs, fights bronchitis and infections

Rhodonite - Treats emphysema, inflammation of bronchial passages, calms coughing

Rose Quartz – Treats asthma, allergies, bronchitis, relieves pressure, detoxifies

Rutilated Quartz - Strengthens the respiratory tract, fights bronchitis, stimulates regeneration of cells and lung tissue

Sardonyx - Heals lungs, reduces mucus, decongests

Shungite- Anti-bacterial, anti-inflammatory, strengthens all body systems, detoxifies and cleanses blood

Vanadinite - Treats asthma and lung congestion, allergies, improves breathing, energizes

Zincite – Decongestion, relieves asthma, bronchitis, strengthens respiratory system, nutrient absorption

Zoisite – Reduces inflammation of the bronchial passages, strengthens respiratory and immune systems

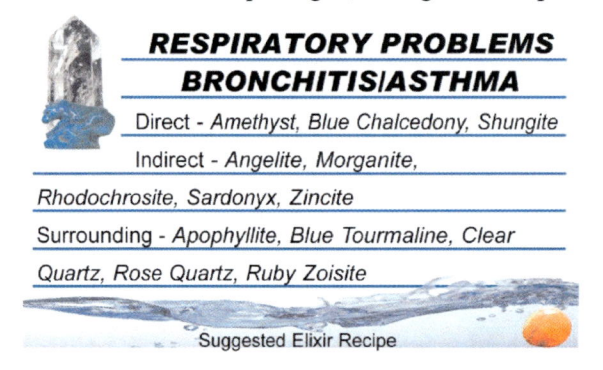

RESPIRATORY PROBLEMS
BRONCHITIS/ASTHMA

Direct - *Amethyst, Blue Chalcedony, Shungite*

Indirect - *Angelite, Morganite, Rhodochrosite, Sardonyx, Zincite*

Surrounding - *Apophyllite, Blue Tourmaline, Clear Quartz, Rose Quartz, Ruby Zoisite*

Suggested Elixir Recipe

CHAPTER SEVEN – Pain, Joints and Bones

"As in nature, as in art, so in grace; it is rough treatment that gives souls, as well as stones, their luster." -Thomas Guthrie

The vibrations of gemstones can reach into our bones and joints to give us relief from pain and aid us in healing. The mineral kingdom is an important part of the whole equation in balancing our physical body. Vitamins, minerals, water and a positive mind set can give our bodies the tools it needs to combat pain and disease for optimum health. You can use a hematite bracelet or Herkimer diamond to relieve joint or arthritic pain quickly and for a short period of time. Try drinking an herbal tea made with a gemstone elixir to give all-day relief.

HEADACHES/MIGRAINES

Agate – Relieves pressure and tension, calms nerve endings, opens capillaries to relieve pain
Amber - Relieves tension headaches, calms nerves, soothes muscles
Amethyst - Eases headaches and releases tension to eliminate pain
Ametrine - Eases stress and tension headaches
Apache Tear – Releases stress, opens capillaries, soothes pain, relieves vision distortion
Aventurine - Relieves migraine headaches, soothes eyes
Blue Lace Agate – Eases tension, removes excess fluid from the brain
Citrine   - Relieves food-related headaches
Clear Calcite - Reduces tension that causes migraines and visual disturbances
Danburite- Reduces ringing in ears, visual disturbances and pressure
Dendritic Agate – Dilates capillaries and circulatory system to relieve pressure
Dioptase - Alleviates headache and migraine pain
Herkimer Diamond – Tunes down pain quickly, eliminates sight and sound aggravation
Iolite - Alleviates migraine headaches
Jet - Treats migraines, soothes nerves, relieves stress
Kyanite – Relieves headache pain and tension, stimulates electrical impulses, reduces inflammation in brain tissue
Labradorite – Reduces tension and emotional headaches, relieves headache pressure
Lapis Lazuli - Relieves migraine and headache pain
Larimar - Dissolves energy blockages in the head
Lithium Quartz – Migraine prevention and treatment, reduces tension and pain
Magnesite - Relieves pain of headaches, migraines, muscle relaxant
Moonstone - Eases food-related headaches
Opal (Cherry) - Alleviates headaches caused by blockages of third eye
Rhodochrosite - Dilates blood vessels to relieve migraines
Serpentine – Lessens pain, visual disturbances and tension
Smoky Quartz - Relieves headache pain
Sugilite - Relieves headache pain and discomfort
Turquoise - Relieves tension headaches

HEADACHE/MIGRAINE PAIN RELIEF

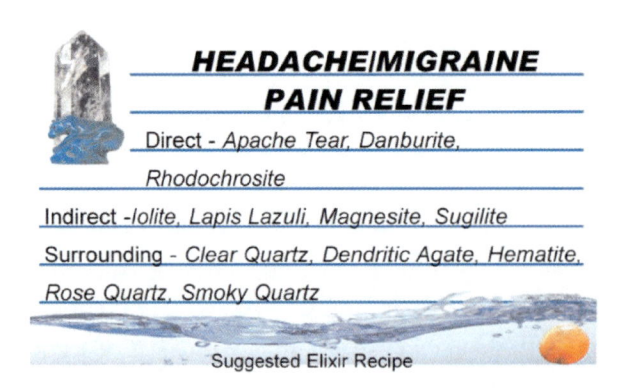

Direct - *Apache Tear, Danburite, Rhodochrosite*
Indirect - *Iolite, Lapis Lazuli, Magnesite, Sugilite*
Surrounding - *Clear Quartz, Dendritic Agate, Hematite, Rose Quartz, Smoky Quartz*

Suggested Elixir Recipe

BACK AILMENTS/SKELETAL SYSTEM

You can fight the symptoms and underlying disease by carrying these stones in your pockets, placing under your pillow or mattress, or wearing jewelry. If you are carrying them in your pocket, be sure to swap them to the other side half way through the day or have one of each stone in each pocket. For example, if you are having problems and pain with the alignment of your spine, keep a tumbled Selenite in each pocket. If you begin to feel fatigued, the pain comes back or you become nauseous, take the Selenite out of your pockets. This is true of any stone or jewelry you may be wearing or carrying around.

Amazonite -Treats tooth decay, osteoporosis, aids and strengthens skeletal system, calcium absorption, reduces and eliminates bone spurs and calcium deposits

Amethyst – Eases pain, strengthens bones, cartilage and skeletal structure, realigns spine for better posture

Apatite - Heals bones, aids cartilage and calcium absorption

Aquamarine – Treats swollen glands, inflammation of the throat, osteoporosis

Aragonite - Restores elasticity in discs, heals bones, reduces pain, aids in calcium absorption

Auralite 23 – Pain relief, muscle relaxant, reduces inflammation

Aventurine - Physical regeneration of muscular system

Azurite - Aids in fighting and reversing cartilage, muscle and tendon damage/disorders, reduces pain and inflammation, helps to align spine and discs, relieves hip and lower back pain, fractures and broken bones

Blue Lace Agate – Relieves pain, works on bone defects, strengthens bones and skeletal system, heals fractures and nails

Calcite -Treats deficiencies, strengthens bones and joints, dissolves calcifications and bone spurs

Carnelian - Treats and alleviates hip and lower back pain/problems, neuralgia

Chrysocolla - Treats bone disease, muscle spasms and cramps, strengthens muscles

Cinnabar - Provides strength and flexibility

Dendritic Agate – Aids in bone alignment, growth and combating osteoporosis

Fluorite –Teeth, bones, balances calcium, removes excess calcium

Fuchsite - Helps with flexibility in musculoskeletal system, muscles spasms, pain relief, spinal alignment

Garnet - Treats back (especially lower back) and spinal disorders, increases energy

Hematite - Aids in spinal alignment, back pain relief, sciatica, heals fractures

Herkimer Diamond – Relieves sciatic pain, restores flexibility, reduces inflammation

Hiddenite - Helps with spinal alignment

Infinite – Eases sore muscles, rebuilds cartilage, combined with Seraphinite is overall healer and rejuvenator
Kyanite – Helps to realign spine, reduces muscle spasms and pain
Labradorite - Treats impacted vertebrae, aids in spinal alignment
Lepidolite - Numbs sciatica and neuralgia, strengthens immune system
Magnetite - Aids cartilage, muscle, tendons, treats lumbago, aligns spine
Malachite – Strengthens back muscles, relieves, tension and pain, reduces inflammation
Obsidian - Treats impacted vertebrae
Peridot - Muscle and tissue regeneration
Rose Quartz - Scars and scar tissue
Selenite - Treats bones, realigns spinal, relieves pain, promotes flexibility
Seraphinite – Reduces pain, inflammation, boosts other gemstone's characteristics, brings body into harmony
Smoky Quartz - Strengthens the back muscles
Super 7 – Clears energy blockages along the spine, releases tension and relaxes muscles

BACKACHE
Direct - *Carnelian, Smoky Quartz,*
Indirect - *Hematite, Infinite, Lepidolite*
Surrounding - *Azurite. Blue Lace Agate, Lapis Lazuli, Malachite, Selenite*

Suggested Elixir Recipe

SCIATICA
Direct - *Carnelian, Herkimer Diamond*
Indirect - *Aragonite, Hematite, Lapis Lazuli, Lepidolite*
Surrounding - *Azurite, Obsidian, Rose Quartz, Selenite, Black & Watermelon Tourmaline*

Suggested Elixir Recipe

BROKEN BONES
Direct - *Amethyst, Carnelian*
Indirect - *Apatite, Apache Tear, Dendritic Agate, Yellow Calcite*
Surrounding - *Aragonite, Obsidian, Rose Quartz, Selenite, Black & Watermelon Tourmaline*

Suggested Elixir Recipe

HERNIATED & IMPACTED DISCS
Direct - *Carnelian, Peridot*
Indirect - *Aragonite, Azurite, Cinnabar, Labradorite, Lepidolite*
Surrounding - *Fuchsite, Obsidian, Selenite, Super 7*

Suggested Elixir Recipe

BONE SPUR REMOVAL
Direct - *Chiastolite, Yellow Obsidian*
Indirect - *Red Calcite, Watermelon Tourmaline*
Surrounding - *Black Tourmaline, Clear Quartz, Sulfur, Tektite*
Suggested Elixir Recipe

HEALTHY BONES OSTEOPOROSIS
Direct - *Amethyst, Aquamarine, Dendritic Agate, Carnelian*
Indirect - *Clear Calcite, Green Calcite*
Surrounding - *Obsidian, Rose Quartz, Selenite, Watermelon Tourmaline*
Suggested Elixir Recipe

JOINT, NERVE & MUSCLE PAIN

Try wearing jewelry to alleviate the pain throughout the day as well as to rebuild and/or maintain your health. Amethyst, Copper, Lapis Lazuli, Hematite and Turquoise bracelets aid in reducing the pain of arthritis and other inflammatory ailments. The combination of bracelets I wear to help me – Amethyst, Seraphinite and Auralite 23. When experiencing a sudden flare-up of pain in one area such as knee, back, elbow, etc., I hold a Magnesite to the area and within a few moments, the pain is gone.

Agate – Heals nervous system, reduces pain and spasms, aids circulatory system

Amazonite – Eliminates muscle spasms and pain

Amber - Absorbs pain, draws disease out of body; alleviates joint problems

Amethyst - Reduces swelling, reduction of pain, combats fatigue, restores general health, increases other gemstone characteristics when combined

Apatite - Treats arthritis and joint problems, improves health

Aquamarine – Pain, inflammation and swelling, water retention

Aragonite – Reduces inflammation, pain of muscles, joints, minor aches, vitamin D deficiencies, restores heat to extremities

Aventurine - Antibacterial, anti-inflammatory, relieves muscle pain and cramps, calms nervous system

Auralite 23 – Pain relief, muscle relaxant, reduces inflammation, heals at cellular level

Azeztulite – Relieves pain, anti-inflammatory, heals and structures cellular disorders, raises pain tolerance and re-energizes

Azurite - Improves health, aids in treatment of arthritis and joint problems

Bloodstone – Anti-inflammatory, circulatory system cleanser and booster, revitalizes and detoxifies

Blue Fluorite - Relieves inflammation, calms nerves, relaxes muscles

Blue Lace Agate - Reduces inflammation and pain, enhances absorption of vitamins and minerals, releases neck tension

Calcite – Sustains and enhances nerve and muscle function, reduces pain due to a calcium deficiency

Carnelian – Treats arthritis, rheumatism, fibromyalgia, nerve pain, balances fluids, cleanses and harmonizes all systems

Chiastolite – Relieves painful rheumatism, soothes nerves, boosts immune system and reduces inflammation

Chrysocolla – Helps relieve arthritis pain, muscle spasms, cramps,

Clear Quartz – Increases energy, purification and detoxification of circulatory system

Copper – Strengthens and purifies circulatory system, reduces inflammation and swelling
Dioptase – Reduces fatigue, boosts immune system, detoxifies, reduces pain and reenergizes T-cells (white blood cell that supports the immune system)
Emerald – Reduces pain and treats rheumatism and other muscle inflammations
Green Calcite - Relieves arthritis pain and muscle constrictions
Carnelian - Heals arthritis and rheumatism, ligament healing
Chrysocolla - Treats arthritis, bone disease, muscle spasms, brings pain relief
Citrine – Reverses muscle and nerve damage, slows down degenerative conditions, strengthens nerves, reduces pain and fatigue
Fluorite - Mobilizes joints, alleviates arthritis, rheumatism, nerve-related pain relief, treats shingles
Garnet - Excellent for treating arthritis and rheumatism, stimulates self-healing
Herkimer Diamond – Pinpoint pain relief, anti-inflammatory, increases flexibility in muscles and joints, calms nerves
Indicolite – Removes excess fluid, finds source of pain and disease, pain management
Infinite/Serpentine – Pain relief, absorption of magnesium and calcium, warms joints and placement area
Iolite – Muscle and pain relaxant, encourages movement through pain, re-energizes, encourages best health, not to give in
Jade – Stimulates blood flow and brings warmth to painful areas, reduces pain and inflammation, allows one to use less pain medication and to manage pain
Jet – Reduces swelling and inflammation, raises body temperature and Kundalini for self-healing
Kyanite – Reduces pain, muscle spasms and meridian blockages
Labradorite – Reduces pain and inflammation related to arthritis and rheumatism, brings warmth to extremities and joints
Lapis Lazuli – Pain relief in all forms, calms nerves and mind to allow healing on all levels
Lepidolite – Aids in transitions of health, encourages change of habits for healing, muscle and nerve relaxant, healing sleep, works on joint pains and disease for better health, boosts immune system
Magnesite – Joint and pinpoint pain relief, antispasmodic, muscle relaxant, balances body temperature
Malachite - Treats arthritis, swollen joints, relieves cramping and pain, lowers blood pressure
Mica (Fuchsite/Muscovite) – Balances potassium levels, alleviates cramps and muscle spasms
Obsidian - Reduces pain of arthritis and rheumatism as well as cramping
Orange Calcite – Encourages pain management and less toxic drug use
Rhodonite - Eases inflammation of joints, treats arthritis, rheumatism, multiple sclerosis, raises energy
Rutilated Quartz – Combats exhaustion and instills energy, heals muscle and tissue damage, eases pain
Selenite- Increases energy, calms nerves and muscle tension, re-aligns bones and joints
Seraphinite – Reduce pain, inflammation, boosts gemstones, brings body into harmony
Smoky Quartz – Relieves pain, strengthens and regenerates nerve and muscle health
Sulfur- Joint pain relief, cools inflammation, energizes body, relieves skin-nerve pain
Topaz – Strengthens and fortifies nerves and muscles, stimulates metabolism
Tourmaline - Provides pain relief and treats arthritis, calms nerves and spasms, regeneration of nerves, combats multiple sclerosis
Turquoise – Strengthens and purifies circulatory system, soothes nerve endings, reduces pain and inflammation

ARTHRITIS
Direct - *Amethyst, Apatite, Seraphinite*
Indirect - *Copper, Green Calcite, Fluorite, Infinite (Serpentine), Magnesite, Rhodonite*
Surrounding - *Azurite, Carnelian, Chrysocolla, Clear Quartz, Garnet, Malachite, Turquoise*

Suggested Elixir Recipe

FIBROMYALGIA
Direct - *Amethyst, Carnelian, Jade, Shungite*
Indirect - *Infinite, Iolite, Rutilated Quartz, Seraphinite*
Surrounding - *Clear Quart, Fluorite, Lepidolite, Rose Quartz, Tourmaline*

Suggested Elixir Recipe

LUPUS
Direct - *Amethyst, Carnelian, Clear Quartz, Shungite*
Indirect - *Amber, Auralite 23, Infinite, Magnesite, Nuumite, Seraphinite, Turquoise*
Surrounding - *Aquamarine, Fluorite, Rose Quartz, Selenite, Sulfur*

Suggested Elixir Recipe

MUSCLE PAIN
Direct - *Amethyst, Blue Lace Agate, Carnelian, Clear Quart*
Indirect - *Lapis Lazuli, Magnesite*
Surrounding - *Copper, Fluorite, Jet, Rose Quartz, Selenite*

Suggested Elixir Recipe

CHAPTER EIGHT – Heart Disease & Chronic Conditions

Chronic conditions affect you all your life and in some cases every minute of every day. The mineral kingdom can help relieve symptoms, as well as treat underlying conditions, to release pain, stress and to strengthen your body's own immune system to fight the disease. Balancing your chakras and treating symptoms can help you deal with the daily battle of many conditions. Anyone suffering from MS should look up the various symptoms they are experiencing to make an elixir that would aid them in their battle. There are so many symptoms and conditions that vary from person to person, it would be impossible to put together a general elixir. Your unique symptoms warrant a unique elixir, and I recommend starting with stones in the joint, nerve and muscle pain section in Chapter 7, as well as some stones in the Chronic Fatigue Syndrome section in this chapter

BLOOD DISEASE/HEART CONDITIONS
(Circulatory System)

Amethyst – Fortifies heart muscle, stabilize blood pressure, beneficial to circulatory system as antiviral, antibacterial

Angelite – Supports heart and circulatory system, cleanses and renews blood cells and vessels

Apatite – Thins blood to prevent heart disease, dissolves clots, cleanses blood

Aragonite – Improves circulation, supports circulatory system, strengthens heart muscle

Aventurine – Strengthens and cleanses circulatory system, prevents heart attack, strokes, lowers cholesterol, balances blood pressure, builds up heart muscle, reduces arteriosclerosis

Bloodstone – Heart muscle damage and irregularity, aids and strengthens circulatory system, balances blood pressure, benefits organs, detoxifies/purifies blood, treats leukemia, cleanses blood of free radicals

Calcite – Strengthens/regulates heart, aids circulatory/blood, lowers cholesterol and blood pressure

Carnelian – Balances body fluids, benefits circulatory system and heart muscle, cleanses arteries, energizes in a slow, steady way, improves absorption of vitamins, minerals and nutrients, detoxifies and cleanses blood

Charoite – Regulates blood pressures, aids in healing damage to heart and circulatory system

Diopside – Prevents heart attacks, repairs damaged heart tissue, cleanses and detoxifies blood, balances blood pressure, battles fatigue and alleviates pain, reduces cholesterol and fat build-up

Dioptase – Balances blood pressure, strengthens heart and circulatory system, aids healing from surgery

Dravite (Brown Tourmaline) – Reduces risk of stroke and heart attacks, rebuilds heart muscle and tissue, balances blood pressure and cholesterol

Emerald – Reduces risk of heart attacks and strokes, regulates insulin, detoxifies blood, control fat levels in body, strengthens heart muscle and tissue

Epidote – Decreases cholesterol, risk of stroke and heart attacks, stabilizes blood sugar and amino acids, supports heart muscle and tissue health

Fluorite – Lowers cholesterol, fights infections, reduces pain

Fulgurite – Reduces plaque and blockages in arteries/veins, increases blood flow and eliminates bacteria in the blood stream

Hematite – Cleanses and detoxifies blood, battles anemia by increasing iron absorption and health of red blood cells, aids in assimilation of vitamins and minerals

Kyanite – Lowers blood pressure, treats infections and strengthens muscles and circulatory system, balances cholesterol

Labradorite – Lowers blood pressure, reduces stress, aids digestive system, respiratory and circulatory systems, reduces pain

Lapis Lazuli – Balances blood pressure, reduces pain, detoxifies blood and boosts immune system

Larimar – Balances cholesterol and removes blockages, nutrient absorption and recovery from illness

Magnesite – Use for angina and other heart problems, relieves stress, prevents heart disease, increases magnesium, calcium and vitamin C absorption, lowers and regulates blood pressure and heart health

Malachite – Lowers blood pressure, detoxifies, purifies blood, reduces angina pain

Mica (Fuchsite/Muscovite) – Lowers and regulates blood pressure, balances pH and potassium levels

Morganite – Prevents heart disease, aids in repairing damage, reduces stress, boosts oxygen in blood cells

Obsidian – Detoxifies blood, lowers blood pressure, aids in dissolving blockages in arteries, cares for circulatory system

Purpurite – Beneficial for heart, circulatory system, balances blood pressure and pulse, stanches bleeding, cleanses and detoxifies blood, fights bacterial infections, re-energizes and rapid healing of bruises

Rhodochrosite – Balances blood pressure, calms rapid heart beat, cleanses circulatory system, expands blood vessels

Rhodonite – Combats autoimmune diseases and blood infections, strengthens immune system

Rose Quartz- Cleanses, strengthens and purifies circulatory system, heart and lungs, eases palpitations

Ruby – Helps heart, circulatory system and blood cells, detoxifies, antibacterial

Ruby Zoisite – Removes toxins from blood, lymphatic system and organs, aids heart and circulatory system, increases blood flow and eliminates blockages/restrictions

Sapphire – Beneficial for circulatory system, blood health, and combats heart and blood disorders, balances blood pressure and cholesterol

Septarian – Aids blood, heart and circulatory system, reduces swelling/bruising, calms rapid heart beat

Sodalite – Lowers blood pressure, cleanses elimination and circulatory systems, builds immune system, strengthens heart muscle and repairs radiation damage

Sulfur – Treats infections, diseases of blood and heart, eliminates bacteria and parasites, reduces swelling

Tourmaline – (Blue, Pink or Red) Aids and strengthens pulmonary system, reduces fluid around heart, treats bacteria infections

Vesuvianite – Reduces risk of stroke and heart attacks, repairs damaged heart tissue, balances blood pressure and cholesterol

Wavellite – Strengthens blood flow, heart, balances white blood cell counts, calms rapid heart beat

Zoisite - Diopside – Repairs heart muscle and tissue damage, balances cholesterol, blood pressure, fat build-up to reduce risk of heart attack and stroke

ANGINA/HEART PALPITATIONS

Direct - *Amethyst, Bloodstone, Rose Quartz, Ruby, Zincite*

Indirect - *Magnesite, Purpurite, Rhodochrosite, Sodalite*

Surrounding - *Clear Quartz, Hematite, Sulfur, Pink Tourmaline, Wavellite, Selenite*

Suggested Elixir Recipe

BALANCING CHOLESTEROL

Direct - *Aventurine, Apatite, Bloodstone, Danburite, Rose Quartz*

Indirect - *Iolite, Magnesite, Morganite, Muscovite, Yellow Topaz*

Surrounding - *Fluorite, Chrysoprase, Howlite, Hematite, Rainbow Jasper, Herkimer Diamond*

Suggested Elixir Recipe

HIGH CHOLESTEROL

Direct - *Amethyst, Bloodstone, Carnelian*

Indirect - *Angelite, Aventurine, Larimar, Obsidian, Septarian, Wavellite*

Surrounding - *Magnesite, Morganite, Sapphire, Ruby Zoisite*

Suggested Elixir Recipe

STRENGTHEN HEART MUSCLE REPAIR

Direct - *Amethyst, Bloodstone, Carnelian, Charoite*

Indirect - *Iolite, Magnesite, Morganite, Muscovite, Yellow Topaz, Diopside or Dioptase, Larimar, Purpurite*

Surrounding - *Magnesite, Rose Quartz, Tourmaline, Wavellite*

Suggested Elixir Recipe

AIDS/HERPES/INFECTIOUS DISEASES

Also see Blood Diseases, Boosting Immune System and other symptoms

Amber – Treats infections, goiters and other throat problems, antibacterial and antifungal

Amethyst - Disinfects, reduces pain, overall health and healing

Angelite – Fights infections, inflammation and fever

Apache Tear – Removes toxins, calms nerves and muscle spasms, aids absorption vitamins and minerals

Aquamarine - Assimilation of vitamins and minerals, cleanses and eliminates toxins

Azeztulite – Cleanses/detoxifies at a cellular level, harmonizes body, mind and spirit for optimal health

Bloodstone - Immune stimulator for acute infections

Carnelian - Boosts energy, metabolism, immune system, elimination system, nutrient absorption and cleanses/detoxifies

Dioptase – Reduces fatigue, boosts immune system and T-cells, detoxifies, reduces pain

Emerald - Strengthens whole body to fight infection, boost energy and eliminate disease

Fluorite - Antibacterial/antiviral, cleanser/detoxifier, treats extreme infections like staph, herpes, ulcers

Hematite – Strengthens circulatory system, cleanses on cellular level

Kyanite – Combats infections, autoimmune diseases and rebuilds immune system

Jade – Strengthens elimination system/kidneys, detoxifies, de-stress, balances alkalinity and body fluids

Jasper – Cleanses and detoxifies the blood and circulatory system, boosts immune system

Magnetite/Lodestone – Boosts compromised immune system to aid in recovery, re-energizes, balances electrolytes

Peridot – Strengthens and balances whole body and mind

Rhodonite – Combats autoimmune diseases and blood infections, strengthens immune system

Shungite- Anti-bacterial, anti-inflammatory, strengthens all body systems, detoxifies and cleanses blood

Sodalite - Boosts immune system, promotes healthy sleeping habits, balances body fluids, lowers blood pressure

Sulfur - Detoxifies, cleanses and re-energizes during illness, reduces swelling, fights infections, reduces allergic reactions

Sunstone – Aids body in taking control and eliminating disease, stimulates and boosts immune system

Zincite – Boosts energy and immune system, works against auto-immune diseases, strengthens elimination system

AIDS/HERPES
Direct - *Amber, Carnelian, Clear Quartz, Shungite*
Indirect - *Bloodstone, Dioptase, Emerald, Fluorite, Jasper, Sulfur*
Surrounding - *Amethyst, Hematite, Rose Quartz, Sunstone, Tourmaline*
Suggested Elixir Recipe

ALZHEIMER'S/DEMENTIA/MEMORY

See Chapter Ten for Studying/Mental Focus)

Amazonite – Removes blockages to energy fields and neural passages, reduces spasms and tics

Apophyllite- Aids focus, memory retention, decision making, clears thought process

Azurite – Removes blockages, plaque and heals damage to brain, releases stress and aids memory

Barite – Assists with fatigue, memory, brain health, detoxification, tension relief

Carnelian – Cleanses, heals and brings harmony of spirit and body, sharpens perspective, memory and decision making

Dendritic Agate- Cleanses, heals and detoxifies circulatory system, allows clear thought and reduces pain

Emerald- Strengthens memory and brain function, detoxifies and promotes positive thought and action

Howlite – Balances calcium, strengthens and stimulates memory, aids with decision making

Kunzite- Aids focus, removes stress, promotes self-acceptance and overcoming obstacles or challenges

Kyanite – Stimulates electrical impulses, reduces inflammation in brain tissue, relieves headache pain

Labradorite – Clears electrical blockages in the brain, reduces plaque build up, increases memory function for motor skills

Lapis Lazuli – Relieves pain and headaches, promotes clear thought, reduces anger, balances emotions

Lepidolite – Combats memory loss and Alzheimer's, boosts immune system, realigns DNA

Mangano - Instills quest for knowledge, brings focus, memory retention, reduces emotional stress while supporting a feeling of self-worth and self-acceptance, aids in proper nutrition

Opal – Strengthens memory, fights infections, boosts immune system

Rose Quartz – Calms emotions, treats Alzheimer's and dementia, heals emotions, alleviates vertigo

Sardonyx – Aids perception, awareness/acuity, fights depression,

Serpentine - Facilitates meditation, brings focus, clarity of thought, enhance intellect, balances emotions
Shungite – Detoxifies, re-energizes, combats fatigue, instills good eating habits, reduces inflammation, benefits memory
Stichtite – Supports, enhances brain and neural pattern, stimulates memory and clear thought process
Sugilite - Combats fatigue, promotes self-confidence, positive thoughts and actions, calms the nerves while eliminating headaches, facilitates memory retention.
Sulfur - Removes negative thinking or destructive tendencies, clarifies thoughts, reasoning skills and decision making,

ALZHEIMER'S
Direct - *Apophyllite, Herkimer Diamond, Rose Quartz, Shungite*
Indirect - *Emerald, Lapis Lazuli, Mangano, Sardonyx*
Surrounding - *Azurite, Labradorite, Moldavite, Stichtite, Sulfur*
Suggested Elixir Recipe

MEMORY/DEMENTIA
Direct - *Apophyllite, Clear Quartz, Rose Quartz*
Indirect - *Amazonite, Barite, Mangano, Sardonyx, Serpentine, Sugilite*
Surrounding - *Amethyst, Azurite, Sulfur*
Suggested Elixir Recipe

CANCER/LEUKEMIA/GROWTHS, TUMORS, FIBROUS MASSES

Alexandrite - Treats side effects of leukemia, aids body in healing itself
Amber – Cleanses, detoxifies, combats illness, raises spirits, elixir soothes protects skin after radiation, prevents infections
Amethyst – Works at a cellular level to combat disorders, brings patient closer to spirit, antibacterial, antifungal boosts immune system, removes pain; helps terminal people to come to terms with mortality and aids in transition through death, overall healing
Ametrine – Detoxifies, aids in recovery, re-energizes, repairs cellular damage, boosts immune system
Auralite 23 – Removes pain, aids in overall healing, reduces foreign masses and cells, imparts energy
Aventurine (Green) - Useful in malignant conditions, brings things back into control, balances pH
Azeztulite – Treats cancer, cellular disorders and inflammation, helps body to reject unhealthy habits, substances, detoxifies and regenerates healthy cells and tissues, aids cancer patients with weight gain, stimulates appetite, will to live and sense of purpose
Azurite – Removes tumors, cleanses and regenerates good cells, detoxifies body
Bloodstone - Shrinks tumors and growths, treats leukemia, cleanses blood of free radicals, balances pH, revitalizes, aids in rebuilding immune system and overall health
Calcite – Fights colon and bone cancer, aids metabolism and balances white blood cells, fights viral and bacterial infections, detoxifies and re-energizes whole body
Carnelian – Cleanses system of free radicals, balances pH, combats prostate and uterine cancers, speeds up healing of bones and marrow, aids in assimilation of vitamins and minerals for overall health
Charoite – Removes disease and aids in healing, re-energizes, aids in metabolism and healing sleep
Chiastolite – Balances pH, boosts and balances immune system, allows restful sleep for body's own defense and healing

Chrysanthemum Stone - Detoxifies, dissolves growths, aids in rebuilding health and immune system
Danburite – Raises Spiritual vibration and optimism, allows terminal patients to cross over and release fears, detoxifies body and all its systems, aids in healing chronic conditions
Dioptase – Works at cellular level restoring/boosting health, activates T-cells, lessens nausea, fights lung/breast cancer
Emerald - Assists healing malignant conditions and recovery, strengthens heart, lungs, bones and liver
Fluorite – Repairs DNA/RNA cells, reduces growths and small tumors, treats infections and skin cancer, pain relief
Infinite – Stronger paired with Seraphinite, pain relief, absorption of nutrients, detoxifies blood and body
Garnet - Works at cellular level, regenerates DNA, absorption of vitamins and minerals, cleanses blood and circulatory system, fights ovarian, colon and vaginal cancers
Howlite – Calms nerves, allows healing sleep, treats skin as well as bone cancer and infections
Jade – Detoxifies body, aids in healing and recovery, balances alkalinity, fights colon and ovarian cancers
Jasper (Green) – Treats lung, breast and skin cancer, detoxifies and re-energizes body's immune system
Red – Fights colon, ovarian and vagina cancer, blood detoxifier, immune stimulant, inhibits tumor growth
Lapis Lazuli- Fights mouth, throat, lung and breast cancer, relieves pain, heals/detoxifies and strengthens immune system
Magnesite – Relieves pain, increases the body's natural healing ability, fights bone cancer, detoxifies body, controls pH balance
Malachite - Treats growths and tumors, realigns DNA, boosts immune system
Mica (Fuchsite/Muscovite) – Balances pH and potassium levels, detoxifies blood, aids kidneys in elimination poisons
Mookaite – Aids in treatment of leukemia and blood disorders, detoxifies, strengthens immune system
Obsidian – Treats prostate cancer and reduces inflammation and enlargement
Prehnite - Stabilize malignancy and aids body in healing naturally, boosts immune system and metabolism
Petalite - Benefits cells, aids with treatment of cancer, enhances connection with angels
Rhodonite – Lung, breast cancer treatment, pain relief, strengthens lungs and heart, aids in recovery from surgery, combats autoimmune diseases and blood infections, strengthens immune system
Rose Quartz –Detoxifies and strengthens immune, respiratory and circulatory systems, fights lung, breast, throat and skin cancer, strengthens organs and boosts metabolism
Shungite - Slows cancer growth, removes bacteria, toxins and heavy metals, boosts immune system
Sodalite - Treats radiation illnesses, nausea, boosts immune system, cools fevers, detoxifies, works again throat and lung cancers
Smoky Quartz - Helps radiation and chemotherapy illnesses/issues, aids nutrient absorption, pain relief
Snowflake Obsidian - Helps to limit the spread of cancer cells, detoxifies/cleanses blood, lymphatic and circulatory systems
Sugilite - Purifies lymphatic, circulatory and immune systems, calms fears, instills hope, gives loving support and channels healing energy
Sulfur - Shrinks fibrous masses, detoxifies immune system, draws out infections
Super 7- Increases body's natural healing abilities, boosts metabolism and absorption, detoxifies at cellular level, brings physical body and energy into harmony

Tangerine Quartz – Aids in recovery after surgery, cleanses and boosts immune system, re-energizes and instills hope

Turquoise – Relieves pain, benefits immune system, combats viral infections at cellular level, heals skin damage, detoxification

Unakite – Aids in recovery of surgery or medical trauma, boosts immune system, heals skin, boosts metabolism

Zincite - Combats free radicals, regulates hormones, balances pH, aids with digestion and metabolism, assimilation of proteins

BONE CANCER
Direct - *Amethyst, Carnelian, Shungite*
Indirect - *Azeztulite, Auralite 23, Clear Calcite, Howlite, Magnesite, Prehnite, Super 7*
Surrounding - *Clear Quartz, Rose Quartz, Selenite, Turquoise, Black Tourmaline*

Suggested Elixir Recipe

BREAST CANCER
Direct - *Amethyst, Carnelian, Rose Quartz, Shungite*
Indirect - *Auralite 23, Azeztulite, Green Jasper, Prehnite, Rhodonite, Super 7*
Surrounding - *Azurite, Bloodstone, Snowflake Obsidian, Sugilite, Sulfur*

Suggested Elixir Recipe

COLON/OVARIAN CANCER
Direct - *Amethyst, Carnelian, Obsidian, Shungite*
Indirect - *Aventurine, Auralite 23, Azeztulite, Red Calcite, Super 7*
Surrounding - *Clear Quartz, Garnet, Jade, Rose Quartz, Snowflake Obsidian*

Suggested Elixir Recipe

LEUKEMIA
Direct - *Ametrine, Bloodstone, Carnelian, Shungite*
Indirect - *Aventurine, Auralite 23, Azeztulite, Charoite, Mookaite, Sugilite, Super 7*
Surrounding - *Amethyst, Azurite, Clear Quartz, Rose Quartz, Turquoise*

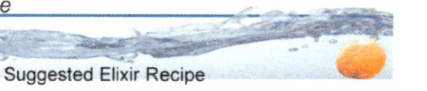

Suggested Elixir Recipe

LUNG CANCER
Direct - *Amethyst, Carnelian, Shungite*
Indirect - *Auralite 23, Azeztulite, Dioptase, Green Jasper, Lapis Lazuli, Rhodonite, Sodalite, Super 7*
Surrounding - *Clear Quartz, Infinite, Rose Quartz, Seraphinite*

Suggested Elixir Recipe

LYMPHOMA
Direct - *Ametrine, Carnelian, Shungite*
Indirect - *Amber, Auralite 23, Aventurine, Azeztulite, Chiastolite, Super 7*
Surrounding - *Amethyst, Clear Quartz, Infinite, Rose Quartz, Seraphinite, Sugilite*

Suggested Elixir Recipe

SKIN CANCER
Direct - *Amethyst, Carnelian, Shungite*
Indirect - *Amber, Auralite 23, Azeztulite, Fluorite, Howlite, Super 7*
Surrounding - *Bloodstone, Clear Quartz, Rose Quartz, Sulfur, Turquoise*

Suggested Elixir Recipe

SURGERY SIDE EFFECTS
Direct - *Ametrine, Carnelian, Bloodstone, Danburite*
Indirect - *Amber, Jade, Malachite, Rhodonite, Unakite*
Surrounding - *Amethyst, Rose Quartz, Clear Quartz, Selenite*

Suggested Elixir Recipe

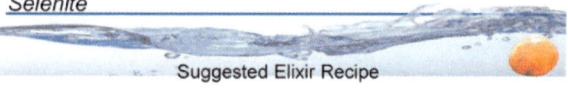

RADIATION SIDE EFFECTS
Direct - *Amethyst, Blue Lace Agate, Carnelian, Shungite, Smoky Quartz*
Indirect - *Lepidolite, Sodalite, Super 7*
Surrounding - *Clear Quartz, Fluorite, Morganite*

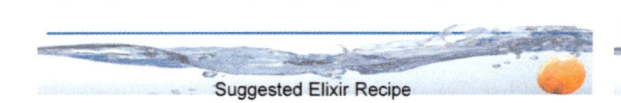

Suggested Elixir Recipe

CHEMOTHERAPY SIDE EFFECTS
Direct - *Amethyst, Carnelian, Citrine, Shungite, Smoky Quartz*
Indirect - *Iolite, Jade, Red Jasper*
Surrounding - *Azurite, Clear Quartz, Danburite, Rose Quartz*

Suggested Elixir Recipe

CHRONIC FATIGUE SYNDROME (CFS)

Amber – Promotes positive mental state and patience, calming influence, mood uplifter, memory aid

Amethyst - Reduces swelling, reduction of pain, combats fatigue, restores general health

Ametrine – Balances enzymes and sugars, antibacterial, strengthens eyes and circulation, rebalance physical body, combats fatigue and depression, re-energizes

Apache Tear – Grounds spirit, cleanses and detoxifies, releases guilt, fear and fights depression

Apatite (Yellow) - Treats pain of joints and muscles, encourages healthy eating and sleeping habits, balances emotional, physical and mental elements, balances activity levels

Auralite 23 - Restores energy, boosts metabolism, increases memory, reduces pain

Barite – Cleanses and rebalances chakras, supports memory, boosts vitality, detoxifies, fights addiction and depression

Bloodstone – Revitalizes/re-energizes, combats exhaustion, detoxifies, supports immune, circulation, digestive and adrenal systems

Bixbite - Promotes self-healing, stamina and vitality, enhances metabolism and immune system

Calcite (Yellow, Orange or Red) Increases energy, uplifts emotions, rekindles will, fights depression, relieves pain

Carnelian – Stimulates life force, metabolism, revitalizes, cleanses, detoxifies, relieves pain/inflammation

Citrine – Restores energy, rebalances emotional, physical and spiritual bodies, balances hormones and fights fatigue

Clear Quartz – Cleanser, detoxifier, purifier, re-energizer, boosts characteristics of other stones, raises vibration and mood

Copper – Energizes, aids iron and nutrient absorption

Danburite – Raises vibration, purifies and re-energizes on spiritual level, fights chronic fatigue
Dioptase – Reduces fatigue, boosts immune system, detoxifies, reduces pain and activates T-cells
Infinite/Serpentine – Pain relief, muscle relaxation, boosts metabolism, re-energizes and rebalances physical and emotional bodies
Garnet – Raises kundalini, rebalances root chakra, re-energizes, regenerates cells and restores body systems to optimal health
Hematite – Aids metabolism, nutrient absorption (iron in particular), memory, calms emotions, relaxes body for a good sleep
Kyanite – Lowers pain, fights infections, relaxes muscles, re-energizes, aids memory
Larimar – Promotes self-healing, revitalizes, supports immune, digestive and respiratory systems, releases pain and blockages
Lepidolite – Relieves exhaustion and pain, promotes self healing, strengthens immune system and vitality
Magnesite – Pain relief, mineral absorption, mood uplifter, detoxifier, memory booster, headache relief
Ruby – Stimulates energy, adrenal, digestive and circulatory systems, boosts immune system, combats exhaustion
Septarian – Aids body in healing and re-energizing itself, boosts metabolism and memory, reduces inflammation and pain
Shungite – Detoxifies, re-energizes, combats fatigue, instills good eating habits, reduces inflammation, benefits memory
Super 7- Aids body in rebalancing, re-energizing and heal itself on all levels, allows body to relax and sleep deeply
Tiger Eye - Raises energy, fights depression, allow you to see deeper into self for cause of disease
Tourmaline – Fights chronic fatigue and negativity, removes blockages, re-establishes good health and habits
Zincite – Raises energy, balances root chakra, increases metabolism and boosts immune system, battles chronic fatigue

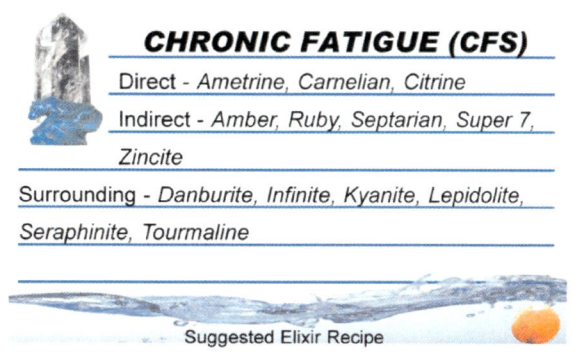

CHRONIC FATIGUE (CFS)
Direct - *Ametrine, Carnelian, Citrine*
Indirect - *Amber, Ruby, Septarian, Super 7, Zincite*
Surrounding - *Danburite, Infinite, Kyanite, Lepidolite, Seraphinite, Tourmaline*

Suggested Elixir Recipe

CROHN'S DISEASE, COLITIS & IBS
Also see Gallbladder/Liver
Agate – Aids digestion and nutrient absorption, improves immune and lymphatic systems
Amethyst – Anti-inflammatory, anti-bacterial, boosts immune and digestive systems, overall healing
Apatite – Aids in production of bile, strengthens elimination and digestive systems, reduces inflammation,

Blue Lace Agate – Cools inflammation, releases tension, releases stress
Calcite – Treats Crohn's, IBS, gallbladder and digestive problems, energizes, reduces fatty build up in liver
Carnelian – Aids, cleanses and strengthens digestive and elimination systems, balance metabolism
Cherry/Pink Opal – Treats colitis, muscle spasm and tension, cleanses and balances base chakra
Fluorite – Reduces cramping and symptoms of colitis, calms inflammation in digestive tract
Infinite/Serpentine – Pain relief, muscle relaxation, boosts metabolism, re-energizes and rebalances physical and emotional bodies
Magnesite – Reduces stress, prevents heart disease, increases magnesium, calcium and vitamin C absorption, pain relief, detoxification, aids digestive and elimination systems
Red Jasper – Treats digestive disorders, calms inflammation, gastritis and bloating, enhances metabolism and nutrient intake, strengthens circulatory and digestive systems
Shungite- Anti-bacterial, anti-inflammatory, boosts immune and digestive systems, detoxifies and strengthens fluids/blood
Strawberry Quartz – Reduces inflammation and mucous output, increases energy
Super 7 – Calms digestive and elimination systems, boosts metabolism, stimulates body's immune system and self-healing

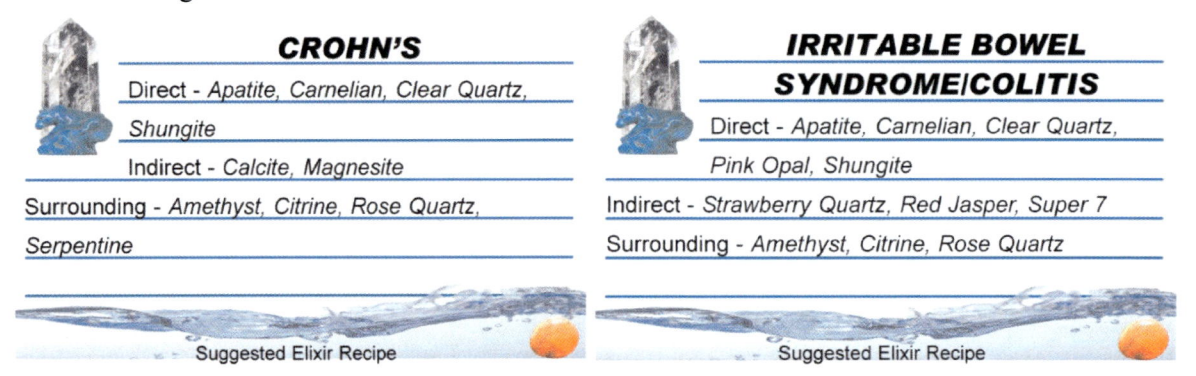

CROHN'S
Direct - *Apatite, Carnelian, Clear Quartz, Shungite*
Indirect - *Calcite, Magnesite*
Surrounding - *Amethyst, Citrine, Rose Quartz, Serpentine*
Suggested Elixir Recipe

IRRITABLE BOWEL SYNDROME/COLITIS
Direct - *Apatite, Carnelian, Clear Quartz, Pink Opal, Shungite*
Indirect - *Strawberry Quartz, Red Jasper, Super 7*
Surrounding - *Amethyst, Citrine, Rose Quartz*
Suggested Elixir Recipe

DIABETES

See also blood disease

Agate – Cleanses, balances, strengthens and stimulates the digestive and circulatory systems, as well as the pancreas
Amber – Stimulate enzymes and reduces sugars, aids pancreas, strengthens organs, balances navel chakra
Amethyst – Balances enzymes and sugars, antibacterial, strengthens eyes and circulation, rebalance physical body
Ametrine – Detoxifies, aids/strengthens cells, organs and physical systems, reduces stress, fatigue, and energizes
Apache Tear – Treats sugar imbalance and transmutes toxins, enhances metabolism, emotional stress
Apatite (Yellow) – Raises metabolism, encourages healthy eating habits, suppresses hunger and cravings
Aquamarine – Strengthens pancreas, balances sugar levels, cleanses blood and flushes excess sugar, breaks down carbohydrates
Azurite – Cleanses blood, stimulates pancreas, balances and aids production of insulin

Barite –Eliminates and transmutes excess sugar, strengthens pancreas, balances insulin levels, increases metabolism, rebalances all chakras, aids in will-power and creating healthy habits
Bloodstone – Cleanses, detoxifies, strengthens and revitalizes organs, blood and circulatory system, treats infections and diabetes
Carnelian – Supports organs, digestive and elimination system, cleanses blood, aids metabolism and absorption of nutrients, balances body fluids, re-energizes
Charoite – Heals, strengthens, revitalizes pancreas, liver, heart and balances blood sugar levels, raises optimism, releases fears
Chiastolite – Heals gout, removes toxins, balances fluid levels and white blood cell levels, aids immune and circulatory systems
Chrysocolla - Cleanses blood, removes disease, regulates insulin levels, strengthens/regenerates pancreas
Chrysoprase – Reduces uric acid, treats gout, aids digestive and elimination systems, purifies and detoxifies blood, increases Vitamin C absorption
Clear Quartz – Cleanses and purifies blood, balances sugar levels, aids in reducing Type 2 health hazards which can lead to insulin injections, re-energizes
Diopside –Balances blood sugar and insulin production, balances fat levels in the body, controls appetite
Emerald – Combats/reduces risk diabetes, regulates insulin, detoxifies blood, aids pancreas and insulin production, control
Epidote – Balances insulin, aids pancreas, maintains sugar levels, reduces risk of diabetes
Infinite – Muscular pain relief, cramps, balances sugar, strengthens pancreas, combined with Seraphinite is overall healer and rejuvenator
Jade – Detoxifies and strengthens elimination and digestive systems, balances fluid levels and metabolism, protects and improves health of spleen and pancreas
Kyanite – Balances insulin output and sugar levels, reduces fat build-up, prevents diabetes
Labradorite – Balances blood sugars, regulates metabolism, benefits digestive, respiratory and circulatory systems, fights gout
Malachite - Aids pancreas, spleen, liver, insulin production and balance, reduces toxins, works on DNA and cellular diseases
Moonstone – Strengthens elimination and digestive systems, balances fluid levels and metabolism
Nuummite – Balances insulin, strengthens pancreas, slows degeneration, aids in healthy lifestyle changes
Opal - Purifies blood, regulates insulin, treats blood disorders
Peridot – Beneficial for the pancreas, spleen and circulatory system, aids metabolism
Red Jasper – Aids lower organs, cleanses and strengthens circulatory system, treats
Rhodonite – Balances body fluids, aids red blood cells, treats infections and autoimmune diseases
Sapphire - Calms overactive organs/systems, treats blood disorders, balance insulin production
Sardonyx – Detoxifies the elimination, circulatory and digestive systems, balances fluid levels, aids absorption of nutrients
Serpentine/Infinite/Atlantasite – Works on hypoglycemia and diabetes, cleanses the blood, balances insulin levels, beneficial for pancreas
Super 7- Aids physical body on all levels by allowing body to healing itself, also works at cellular level
Tiger Eye – Balances blood sugar and fluid levels, benefits pancreas and elimination system, aids metabolism, re-energizes

Vesuvianite – Reduces diabetes risk, regulates insulin production and sugar levels, detoxifies blood, aids pancreas
Zincite – Benefits all organs and systems, aids immune system, re-energizes, detoxifies, supports better eating and habits

DIABETES
Direct - *Aquamarine, Carnelian, Citrine, Red Jasper*
Indirect - *Chrysocolla, Emerald, Opal, Serpentine*
Surrounding - *Amethyst, Clear Quartz, Jade, Malachite, Super 7, Tiger Eye, Zincite*
Suggested Elixir Recipe

EPILEPSY/SEIZURES

Agate (Moss/Turitella) - Enhances brain health and function, improves concentration, harmony of body and mind
Amazonite – Removes blockages to energy fields and neural passages, reduces spasms and seizures
Amethyst – Calms nerves, anti-inflammatory, aids general health, harmony in body, mind and spirit, protection
Apache Tear – Removes toxins, calms nerves and muscle spasms, reduces distress, better self image
Azurite – Reduces anxiety, calms nerves and muscle spasms, enables restructuring of cells for self-healing
Chrysocolla – Quiets muscle spasms, treats blood disorders, detoxifies and cleanses, boosts metabolism
Clear Quartz – Cleanse, purify and realign brain for optimum neural and electrical impulses
Emerald - Strengthens and balances brain function, detoxifies, promotes positive neural pathways
Fluorite – Lessens stress and soothes the nerves, brings harmony to mind and body, reduces muscle rigidity
Lapis Lazuli – Releases pain, lessens seizures, promotes good diet and health habits to prevent seizures
Malachite – Treats/prevents seizures, vertigo and strengthens optic nerve, lowers blood pressure
Selenite – Aids brain function, brings harmony in brain activity and electrical impulses to prevent seizures
Septarian (Dragonstone) – Allows body to balance it own energies to heal itself, calms spasms and twitches
Sugilite - Treats headache pain and seizures, calms nerves, enhance focus and clarity, balances neural networks
Tourmaline - Decreases rigidity in nerves and muscles, calms stress and negativity
Zincite – Treats seizures and epilepsy, fights auto-immune diseases, re-energizes and boosts metabolism

EPILEPSY/SEIZURES
Direct - *Apache Tear, Clear Quartz, Sugilite*
Indirect - *Amazonite, Emerald, Fluorite, Lapis Lazuli, Selenite*
Surrounding - *Rose Quartz, Septarian, Tourmaline*

Suggested Elixir Recipe

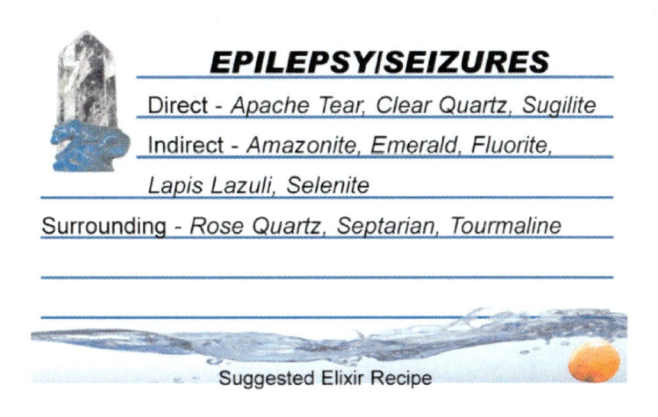

PARKINSON'S DISEASE/TREMORS/NERVE DAMAGE
Also look up individual symptom treatments.
Amazonite – Removes blockages to energy fields and neural passages, reduces spasms and tics
Aragonite – Calms spasms and twitches, boosts immune system, reduces pain, expands veins, capillaries, purifies blood
Azurite – Reduces anxiety, calms nerves and muscle spasms, enables restructuring of cells for self-healing especially in the brain
Chiastolite – Repairs chromosome damage, balances and strengthens immune system, treats muscles and combats paralysis
Chrysocolla – Quiets muscle spasms, treats blood disorders, detoxifies and cleanses, boosts metabolism
Clear Quartz – Cleanse, purify and realign brain for optimum neural and electrical impulses
Kyanite – Reduces muscle spasms, balances electrical impulses, reduces inflammation in brain tissue
Nuummite – Treats symptoms, slows degenerative progression, reenergizes vitality, calms nervous system
Opal – Slows Parkinson's progression, strengthens memory, fights infections, boosts immune system
Orange Calcite – Instills sense of hope/childlike wonder, mood uplifter, re-energizes body, calms stress
Rose Quartz – Treats symptoms of Parkinson's, heals emotions, alleviates vertigo, cleanses and detoxifies entire body
Scolecite – Balances serotonin levels, reduces stress, brings harmony and balance between mind, body and soul, instills hope
Septarian (Dragonstone) – Allows body to balance own energies to heal, calms spasms and twitches
Stichtite – Treats Parkinson's, calms mind and nerves, balances brain fluids and electrical impulses
Super 7 – Aids the body in healing itself, balances chakras, brings feeling of peace
Tourmaline (Green/Watermelon) – Decreases rigidity in nerves and muscles, regenerates and strengthens body, promotes healing sleep, calms stress and negativity

PARKINSON'S

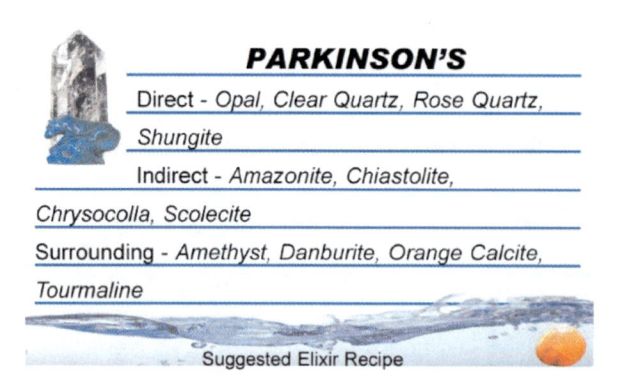

Direct - *Opal, Clear Quartz, Rose Quartz, Shungite*

Indirect - *Amazonite, Chiastolite, Chrysocolla, Scolecite*

Surrounding - *Amethyst, Danburite, Orange Calcite, Tourmaline*

Suggested Elixir Recipe

RAYNAUD'S DISEASE

Aragonite – Stops muscle spasms, bring warmth to extremities, improves circulation
Bloodstone – Strengthens circulatory system, reduces tingling and cold in toes and fingers
Carnelian – Supports organs, digestive, circulatory and elimination systems, metabolism, re-energizes
Dendritic Agate – Reduces pain, opens capillaries for blood flow and warmth
Magnesite – Assists veins, capillaries and blood flow, reduces pain, aids circulatory system
Moonstone – Reduces pain, increases circulation, regulates body temperature, eliminates fever and chills

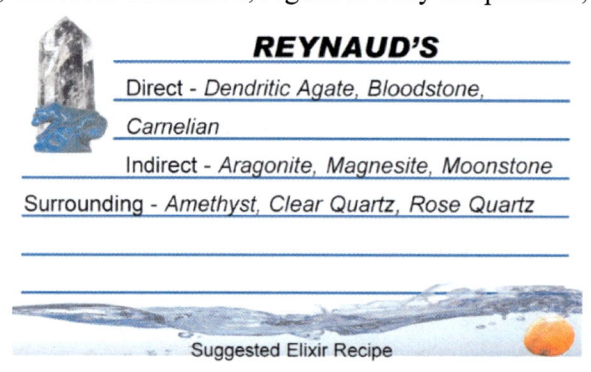

REYNAUD'S

Direct - *Dendritic Agate, Bloodstone, Carnelian*

Indirect - *Aragonite, Magnesite, Moonstone*

Surrounding - *Amethyst, Clear Quartz, Rose Quartz*

Suggested Elixir Recipe

CHAPTER NINE – Eyes, Ears, Skin

While gemstones cannot correct vision or restore hearing, they can enhance the health of these organs. These minerals work to strengthen these senses, working with your body's own natural healing abilities. According to my eye doctor, I had fast growing cataracts, and I believe that by working with a few gemstones, I was able to slow down the rate of cataract growth. I have no scientific proof, but I do feel that a combination of gemstones (minerals) allowed me to delay the surgery for a short time. For skin cancer, please see the recipe under Cancer/Growths in Chapter Eight.

EYES/VISON
Agate (Blue Lace Agate) – Reduces eye irritation, inflammation, soothes burning sensation, dry eye
Amber – Lessens itching and burning, eye ducts, tears, dry eye
Amethyst – Relieves tired eyes, lessens burning and itching, strengthens overall eye health
Angelite/Blue Celestite – Restores perspective, relieves irritation and dryness, clarifies vision
Apophyllite – Rejuvenate and refresh tired eyes, clears vision
Aquamarine – Improves vision, relieves eye strain, refreshes eyes and tear ducts
Azeztulite – Relieves eye pressure, improves vision, strengthens and heals cornea, improves focus
Blue Lace Agate – Soothes tired and sore eyes, cools burning and itching
Blue Chalcedony – Treats glaucoma by reducing eye pressure, reduces inflammation, calms pain
Calcite (Clear) - Benefits the eyes and clears vision, sharpens focus
Carnelian - Cleanses and refreshes eyes, strengthens optic nerve, muscles, capillaries and veins, fights infections
Clear Quartz/Herkimer Diamond – Strengthens weakened vision, soothes burning eyes, overall health
Diamond – Clears focus, treats glaucoma, fights allergies, balances eye fluid
Emerald – Sharpens focus, soothes the eyes, calms twitching, soothes skin around eyes
Fire Agate – Aids night vision and strengthens eyes, aids in correcting eye ailments
Labradorite – Sharpens vision, slows down degeneration and cataracts, eliminate eye disease
Malachite – Strengthens optic nerve, fights allergies, infections and vertigo, lowers blood pressure
Moonstone – Aids night vision, stops degradation of vision, heals tired eyes
Nuummite – Slows eyesight degradation, rebuilds tissue, soothes burning/tired eyes, calms nerves
Obsidian (Apache Tear/Mahogany) – Overall eye health, sharpens focus, relaxes spasms
Opal – Combats dry eye syndrome, strengthens muscles, heals tears in cornea
Peridot – Strengthens optic nerve, cornea, capillaries and veins, fights eye diseases
Rhodochrosite – Heals the surface as well as the layers of the eye, treats cataracts and corneal tears, aids in recovery from retinal surgery, infections and restores optimum sight
Rhodonite – Quick recovery from temporary vision loss or eye surgery, overall strengthening of vision and health of eye
Sapphire – Treats double vision, strengthens eyes, capillaries and detoxifies
Sardonyx – Repairs and strengthens sensory organs
Smoky Quartz – Clears vision, purifies eyes and tear ducts, treats infections, combats dry eye syndrome
Tiger Eye – Improves night vision, depth perception and eye strength
Turquoise – Slows growth of cataracts, aids in improving vision

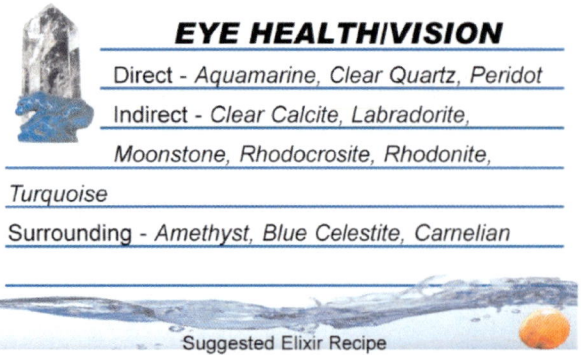

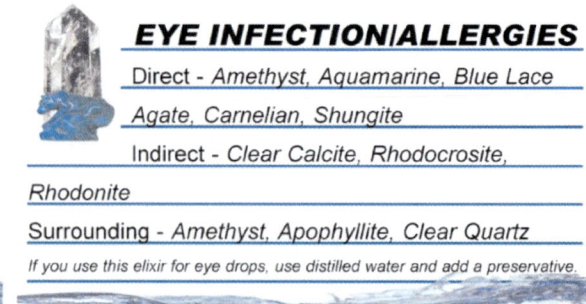

EYE HEALTH/VISION
Direct - *Aquamarine, Clear Quartz, Peridot*
Indirect - *Clear Calcite, Labradorite, Moonstone, Rhodocrosite, Rhodonite, Turquoise*
Surrounding - *Amethyst, Blue Celestite, Carnelian*

Suggested Elixir Recipe

EYE INFECTION/ALLERGIES
Direct - *Amethyst, Aquamarine, Blue Lace Agate, Carnelian, Shungite*
Indirect - *Clear Calcite, Rhodocrosite, Rhodonite*
Surrounding - *Amethyst, Apophyllite, Clear Quartz*

If you use this elixir for eye drops, use distilled water and add a preservative.

Suggested Elixir Recipe

HEARING

Amethyst - Reduces excess noise, quiets the mind, improves overall health of ears
Angelite/Blue Celestite – Combats ear infections and hearing disorders, relaxes mind and muscles
Azurite - Lessens the noise/chatter of tinnitus
Calcite – Strengthens the bones, improves conductivity of sounds
Carnelian – Treats infections, cleanses and purifies, amplifies sounds
Celestite - Treats hearing conditions, tinnitus, improves clarity of sound
Clear Quartz/Herkimer Diamond – Amplifies sound, boosts hearing, detoxifies and fights infections
Danburite - Removes the high pitch of tinnitus and aids in healing this condition, quiets the mind
Dioptase – Treats vertigo and inner ear infections/disorders
Fluorite – Calms stress, boosts hearing, helps to reduce background noise
Lapis Lazuli – Improves hearing, reduces pain, lowers blood pressure, combats inner ear imbalances and infections
Magnetite – Reduces inflammation, calms and heals muscles, relieves inner ear pressure and pain
Rhodochrosite – Calms nerves and stress, lowers background noise, fights infections and reduces fluid
Rhodonite – Reduces hypersensitivity to noise, amplifies hearing, protects and strengthens bones, treats inflammation and infection
Sardonyx – Repairs and strengthens sensory organs – especially hearing
Serpentine – Cleanses, detoxifies and treats infections, boosts immune system, reduces pressure and pain
Tiger Eye – Balances fluids, strengthens inner ear bones, reduces stress, amplifies sound

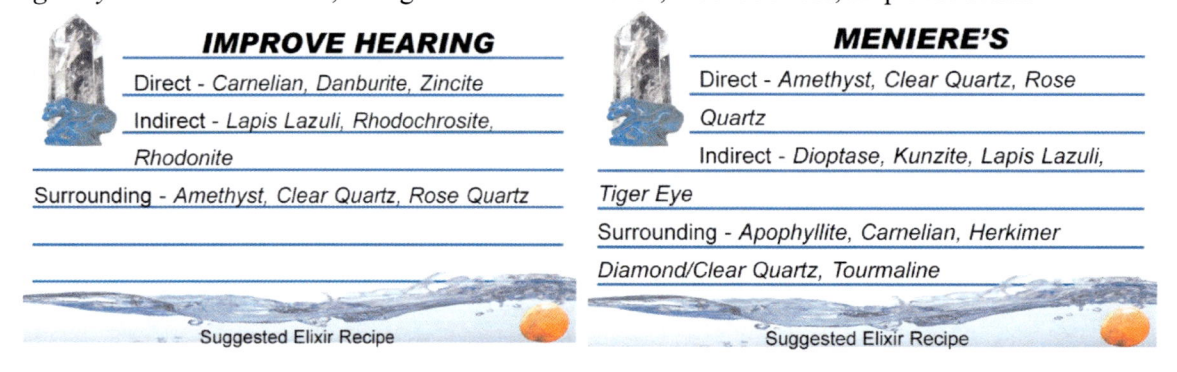

IMPROVE HEARING
Direct - *Carnelian, Danburite, Zincite*
Indirect - *Lapis Lazuli, Rhodochrosite, Rhodonite*
Surrounding - *Amethyst, Clear Quartz, Rose Quartz*

Suggested Elixir Recipe

MENIERE'S
Direct - *Amethyst, Clear Quartz, Rose Quartz*
Indirect - *Dioptase, Kunzite, Lapis Lazuli, Tiger Eye*
Surrounding - *Apophyllite, Carnelian, Herkimer Diamond/Clear Quartz, Tourmaline*

Suggested Elixir Recipe

TINNITUS

Direct - *Amethyst, Danburite, Shungite*

Indirect - *Rhodochrosite, Rhodonite*

Surrounding - *Apophyllite, Carnelian, Herkimer Diamond/Clear Quartz, Tourmaline*

Suggested Elixir Recipe

SKIN DISORDERS/ALLERGIES

Amber - Boils, blisters, acne, bug bites
Amethyst - Healing, burns, bruises, blisters, welling, acne, eczema, sores/bedsores, antiseptic
Angelite/Blue Celestite – Soothes and repairs skin tissue, anti-inflammatory, reduces pain
Apatite – Aids in the production of collagen, prevents wrinkles
Apophyllite - Rejuvenation/regeneration of skin, allergies, purification
Azurite - Regeneration and treatment of cells, relieves itching
Aventurine -Eczema, cell repair, re-growth and healing, skin eruptions, anti-inflammatory, allergies
Blue Lace Agate –Heals psoriasis, eczema, bed sores, blisters, bruises, shingles, skin ulcers, burns
Calcite - Treats the skin, ulcers, growths and warts
Chrysanthemum - Treats growths and disorders of the skin
Copper – Collagen production, protection from free radicals, strengthens skin, reduces pain
Fluorite – Treats skin disorders, combats acne, blemishes and wrinkles
Galena- Beneficial for skin and hair, absorption of zinc and selenium
Emerald - Skin cancer, ulcers, warts
Iolite – Kills bacteria, detoxification, soothes hot spots and skin irritations such as bug bites
Jasper (Brown) - Cell regeneration, detoxifies, heal skin disorders
Labradorite – Works on psoriasis, eczema, acne and other rashes, relieves itching and pain
Lapis Lazuli - Pain, itching, sores, boils
Lepidolite - Detoxifies, soothes skin and wrinkles, skin allergies
Magnetite - (Lodestone) Stimulates growth and healing, anti-inflammatory
Mica (Fuchsite/Muscovite) – Improves and supports healthy skin
Moonstone - Burns, bites, stings, allergic reactions, degenerative disorders
Moss Agate - Treats fungal and skin infections/disorders (elixir applied to skin), acne, eczema
Peridot - Strengthens & rejuvenates skin cells and tissue
Rhodochrosite- Stress, allergies, infections, ulcers, inflammation, use elixir in poultice
Rose Quartz - Blisters, burns, bruises, shingles, sores, clears complexion and reduces wrinkles
Sapphire - Boils, carbuncles, eczema
Shungite - Eczema, psoriasis, acne or other skin related allergies, eliminates bacteria, nitrates, pesticides, chlorine, fluoride, heavy metals

Smithsonite - Eruptions, acne, disorders, relieves skin problems, promotes skin elasticity

Sulfur – External use only, detoxifier, treats acne, skin eruptions or irritations, aids in production of collagen to prevent wrinkles

Zincite - Heals and strengthens skin, combats free radicals

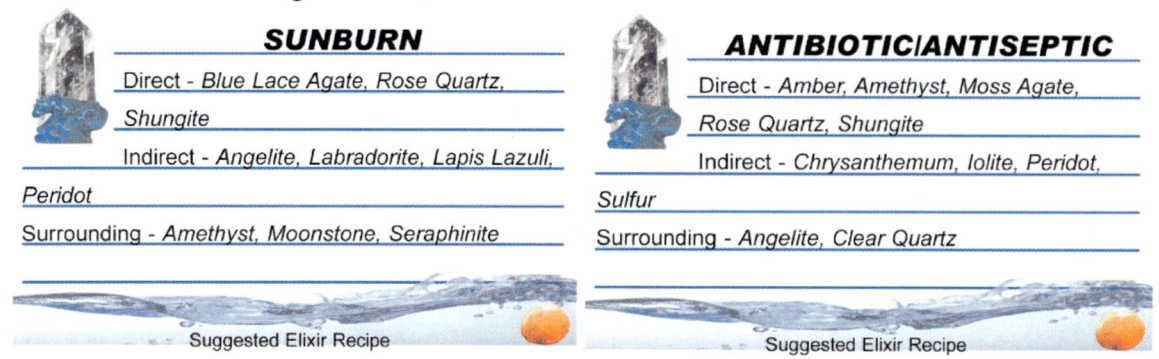

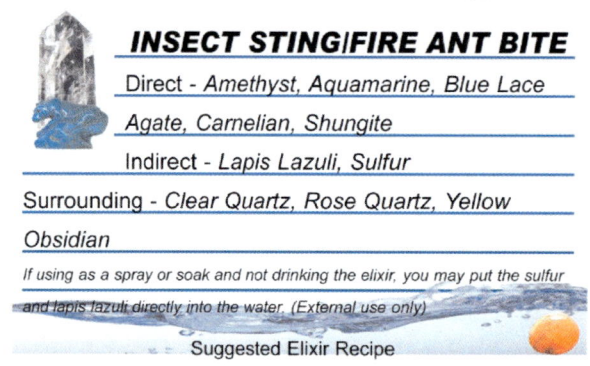

SUNBURN

Direct - *Blue Lace Agate, Rose Quartz, Shungite*

Indirect - *Angelite, Labradorite, Lapis Lazuli, Peridot*

Surrounding - *Amethyst, Moonstone, Seraphinite*

Suggested Elixir Recipe

ANTIBIOTIC/ANTISEPTIC

Direct - *Amber, Amethyst, Moss Agate, Rose Quartz, Shungite*

Indirect - *Chrysanthemum, Iolite, Peridot, Sulfur*

Surrounding - *Angelite, Clear Quartz*

Suggested Elixir Recipe

INSECT STING/FIRE ANT BITE

Direct - *Amethyst, Aquamarine, Blue Lace Agate, Carnelian, Shungite*

Indirect - *Lapis Lazuli, Sulfur*

Surrounding - *Clear Quartz, Rose Quartz, Yellow Obsidian*

If using as a spray or soak and not drinking the elixir, you may put the sulfur and lapis lazuli directly into the water. (External use only)

Suggested Elixir Recipe

CHAPTER TEN – Miscellaneous Recipes

From gemstones for plants to stones for good grades, this chapter addresses many different and unique ways to use gemstones that are not covered anywhere else in this book. Many of these recipes work well as elixirs or sprays. In some cases, just placing the stone in the environment is the best course of action, while in other cases, wearing jewelry or keeping the stones in your pocket will work.

AUTISM

Apatite – Focus, creativity, communication, self-expression, combats frustration, isolation and separation
Apophyllite – Clear communication, calms fears, reduces anxiety, aids focus and decision making
Charoite – Combats frustration and separation, reduces anxiety and obsessive compulsive behavior, increases focus
Danburite – Reconnection, attunement between body, mind and spirit, relaxes rigidity in behavior/body
Hematite – Harmony of body, mind and spirit, self-esteem, confidence, focus, communication, aids daily functioning, grounding
Howlite – Attention, awareness and focus, calms, aids communication, balances emotions, increases social interaction
Kyanite – Aids in building bridges in communication both internally and externally, calms emotions and brings clarity
Obsidian – Grounding, protection, helps getting out of head and more in touch with surroundings, focus
Sardonyx - Increases social interaction, clarity of thought, balances sensitivity, self-expression
Shungite – Purifier, grounding, calming, instills sense of clarity and connection
Smoky Quartz – Removes negativity, protection, grounding, clarity, removes fear, calms, improves concentration
Sugilite - Aids concentration and communication, balances emotions, decreases sensitivity, increases social interaction, awareness

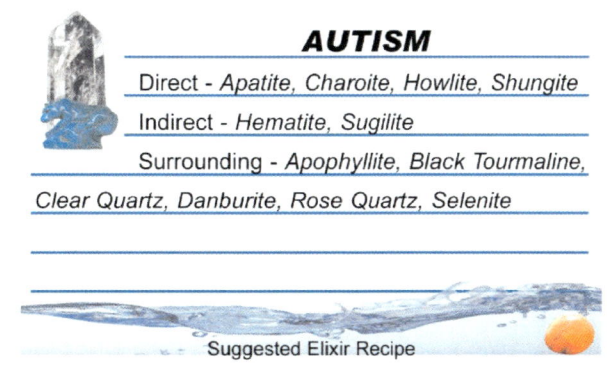

AUTISM

Direct - *Apatite, Charoite, Howlite, Shungite*
Indirect - *Hematite, Sugilite*
Surrounding - *Apophyllite, Black Tourmaline, Clear Quartz, Danburite, Rose Quartz, Selenite*

Suggested Elixir Recipe

DEODORANT
You will want to make a spray or roll on for this recipe. I recommend reapplying this two to three times a day, especially in the summer.

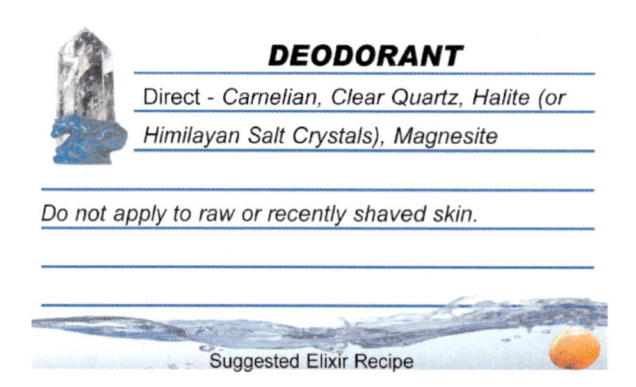

DEODORANT
Direct - Carnelian, Clear Quartz, Halite (or Himilayan Salt Crystals), Magnesite

Do not apply to raw or recently shaved skin.

Suggested Elixir Recipe

EARTH HEALING
Use outside for blessing and/or healing the ground, plants, trees and ponds. Make a spray for indoor meditation and prayer. Use these stones in a mandala or on your altar.

Agate – Establishes a pure connection with nature, fights repression, elevates courage, aids communication, brings harmony to relationships, reduces anger and frustration, combats environmental pollutants

Amber - Encourages growth, pollination and strengthens connection of Heaven and Earth

Aragonite – Promotes conservation, recycling and connection to the earth as well as all living things

Blue Fluorite – Brings deeper peace, understanding difficulties, instill more stability, peace in the world

Chalcedony – Inspires peace and harmony in difficult situations, reduces stress, calms nerves due to weather conditions, instills a sense of compassion, combats poisons and toxicity in nature

Chrysocolla – Fosters balanced energy and environmental harmony, inspires connection with the earth and all beings, reduces negativity and tension, removes guilt and inspires joy

Halite – Cleanses and refreshes air quality, renewal of perspective and compassion, strengthens connection with nature

Jet – Creates a strong Earth to Divine connection, aids in healing, protection

Larimar – Rebalances energies, brings harmony, inspires nurturing and conservation, reconnection with earth, heights spirituality

Malachite – Reduces negativity and tension, balances energy and brings harmony to the environment, inspires connection with nature, guards against radiation, detoxifies and heals the earth

Quartz – Raises awareness and connection to nature and spirit, detoxifies and purifies water, air and earth, calms emotional tension, promotes harmony

Shungite – Purification and detoxification of earth and water, cleanses air of electromagnetic smog and radiation, combats negativity, instills sense of peace, realization of connection to nature/all living beings

Tiger's Eye – Balances emotions and brings harmony to environment, inspires conservation and recycling, compassion and connection to all, encourages integrity in all things

EARTH HEALING
Direct - *Agate, Amethyst, Carnelian*
Indirect - *Amber, Jet, Sodalite*
Surrounding - *Clear Quartz, Rose Quartz, Shungite*

Suggested Elixir Recipe

EDEMA

See also Heart Disease, Infections

Agate – Cleanses and treats infections of the lymphatic system, reduces swelling, boosts the digestive and elimination systems

Amethyst – Strengthens immune, digestive, endocrine and elimination systems, decreases swelling, balances water absorption, releases toxins and fights infections

Angelite – Balances body fluids, releases toxins and excess water, calms swelling and treats infections

Apatite – Eliminates toxins and excess fluids, strengthens digestive system

Aquamarine – Releases excess fluids, encourages flushing out of impurities, strengthens endocrine, digestive and immune systems

Carnelian – Cleanses all systems and balances body fluids, brings body, mind and spirit into harmony

Jasper – Aids in digestion and elimination, reduces swelling and fluid build up, cools infection and allergic reactions

Sulfur - Detoxifies, cleanses and re-energizes during illness, reduces swelling, fights infections, reduces allergic reactions

Zincite – Boosts energy, immune, digestive and elimination systems, reduces fluid build up

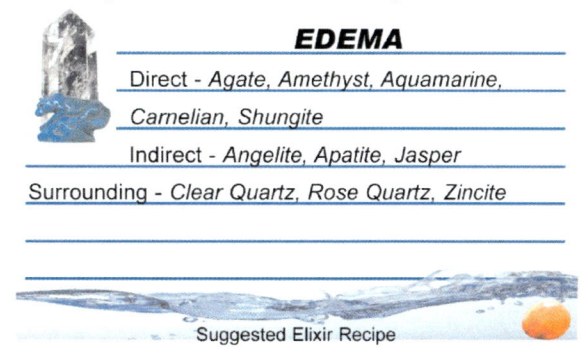

EDEMA
Direct - *Agate, Amethyst, Aquamarine, Carnelian, Shungite*
Indirect - *Angelite, Apatite, Jasper*
Surrounding - *Clear Quartz, Rose Quartz, Zincite*

Suggested Elixir Recipe

ENERGIZING FOOT BATH

After a rough day of work or physical activity, an energizing foot bath will lift your spirits as well as your energy.

ENERGIZING FOOT BATH
Direct - Amethyst, Carnelian, Citrine, Clear Quartz, Garnet, Red Jasper, Yellow Obsidian

Suggested Elixir Recipe

GALLBLADDER/LIVER

Apatite – Aids in producing bile and removal of fatty build-up in the liver
Aventurine – Strengthens and cleanses circulatory, digestive and elimination systems, lowers cholesterol, balances blood pressure
Azurite - Removes tumors, cleanses blood cells, detoxifies body, heals gallbladder, kidney and liver
Bloodstone – Benefits gallbladder, detoxifies/purifies blood, inhibits stone growth, breaks down stones
Calcite – (Orange/Pink) Treats IBS, gallbladder and digestive problems, energizes, cleanses and dissolves calcium deposits/growths
Carnelian – Balances body fluids, benefits circulatory system and gallbladder, improves absorption of vitamins, minerals and nutrients, detoxifies and cleanses blood
Clear Quart – Purifies/detoxifies the blood and organs, provides energy, promotes healthy diet
Charoite – Transmutes negativity, treats liver and elimination systems, reenergizes, detoxifies, heals liver of alcohol abuse, instills sense of duty to help one-self and others, will to live a wholesome life
Danburite – Strengthens, detoxifies and supports liver and gallbladder, benefits all physical, mental and spiritual systems
Fire Agate – Heals stomach, liver, gallbladder, aids elimination, circulation and digestive systems, breaks bad habits
Green Jasper – Eliminates bloating, decreases cravings, cleanses and strengthens liver and digestive tract
Hematite- Aids circulatory and elimination systems, removes self limitations and destructive thoughts, enhances willpower to overcome addictions and compulsions
Iolite – Aids in releasing toxins, boosts immune system and regenerates liver
Larimar – Balances cholesterol and removes blockages, beneficial to major organs
Peridot – Strengthens gallbladder and liver, benefits digestive and elimination systems
Ruby – Detoxifies and boosts immune, circulation, elimination and respiratory systems, liver and spleen
Sapphire – Beneficial for circulatory system, blood health, and combats heart and blood disorders, balances blood pressure and cholesterol

Serpentine – Beneficial to gallbladder, liver, spleen and pancreas, cleanses/detoxifies blood and fluids
Shungite – Cleansing, eliminates toxins, boosts immune and digestive systems, strengthens liver, treats gallbladder and stones
Tourmaline – Breaks down blockages, treats kidney and liver conditions, aids digestive and intestinal disorders

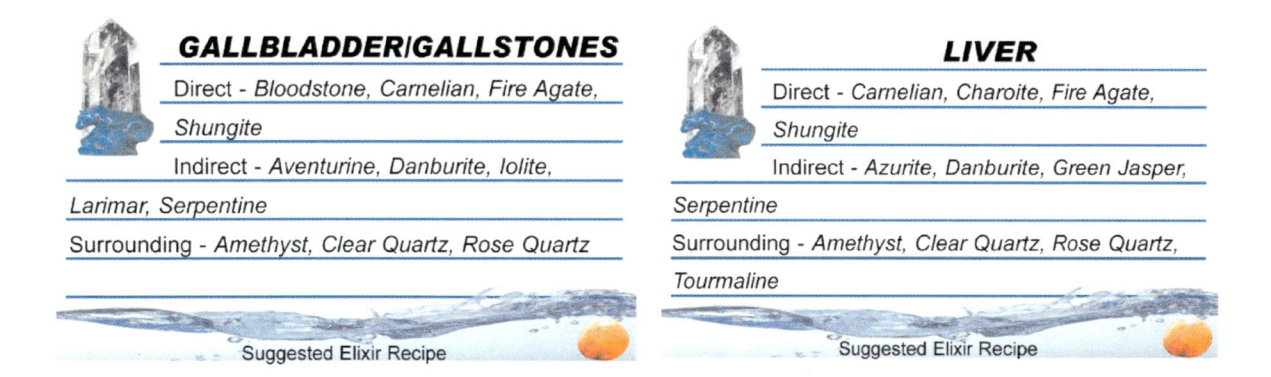

GALLBLADDER/GALLSTONES
Direct - *Bloodstone, Carnelian, Fire Agate, Shungite*
Indirect - *Aventurine, Danburite, Iolite, Larimar, Serpentine*
Surrounding - *Amethyst, Clear Quartz, Rose Quartz*

Suggested Elixir Recipe

LIVER
Direct - *Carnelian, Charoite, Fire Agate, Shungite*
Indirect - *Azurite, Danburite, Green Jasper, Serpentine*
Surrounding - *Amethyst, Clear Quartz, Rose Quartz, Tourmaline*

Suggested Elixir Recipe

HAIR

Copper – Provides melanin for color and health
Galena- Beneficial for hair and skin, absorption of zinc and selenium
Larimar – Conditions hair, aids in absorption of nutrients
Magnetite – Aids hair health and growth
Mica (Fuchsite/Muscovite)- Combats allergies and dandruff, generates shiny, healthy hair
Moonstone – Beneficial for hair health, growth (re-growing) and removes toxins
Turquoise – Healthy hair and color, reduces pollutants, nutrient assimilation
Unakite – Hair growth, health and recovery after illness, detoxifies
Zincite – Increases hair health, aids in growth, adds shine
Zoisite – Aids in hair recovery and growth, especially after trauma or illness

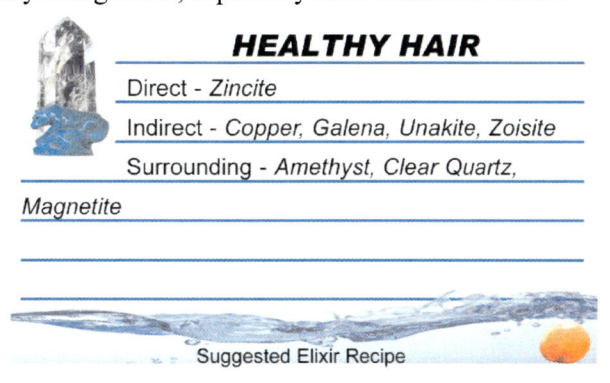

HEALTHY HAIR
Direct - *Zincite*
Indirect - *Copper, Galena, Unakite, Zoisite*
Surrounding - *Amethyst, Clear Quartz, Magnetite*

Suggested Elixir Recipe

IMPOTENCE/LIBIDO

Angelite – Reduces physical drive, redirects energy into spiritual pathways
Apatite – Removes excess energy and overstimulation, balances physical, emotional, spiritual and mental bodies

Aragonite – Circulation to extremities, reduces nervousness, imparts vitality
Blue Lace Agate – Calms, soothes, reduces inflammation and heat, balances sexual drive
Carnelian – Vitality, regulates body fluids, combats impotence, energizes, heals emotions and abuse, restores sexual desire
Clear Quartz- Purifies, energizes, balances, overall healing
Copper – Balances physical and mental states
Fluorite – Increases libido and sexual passion, reduces nervousness and pain
Garnet – Is an aphrodisiac, raises and balances the libido, reduces impotency
Moonstone – Female power, passion
Morganite – Relaxes and reduces stress, combats impotency aids sexual drive and prolongs the experience
Pietersite – Calms physical drive, reduces sexual imbalances
Pyrite – Male power, virility
Red Jasper – Calms emotions, stimulates desire and drive
Ruby- Raises passion and desire, stimulates the sexual organs, instills vitality
Scolecite – Reduces heat, balances emotions, instills rational thought–
Sulfur – Reduces sexual imbalances, calms urges and instills reasoned thought
Sunstone – Increases vitality and sexual drive, instills confidence, energizes and removes inhibitions
Zoisite – Stimulates passion and desire, increases potency and prolongs experience combined with Ruby

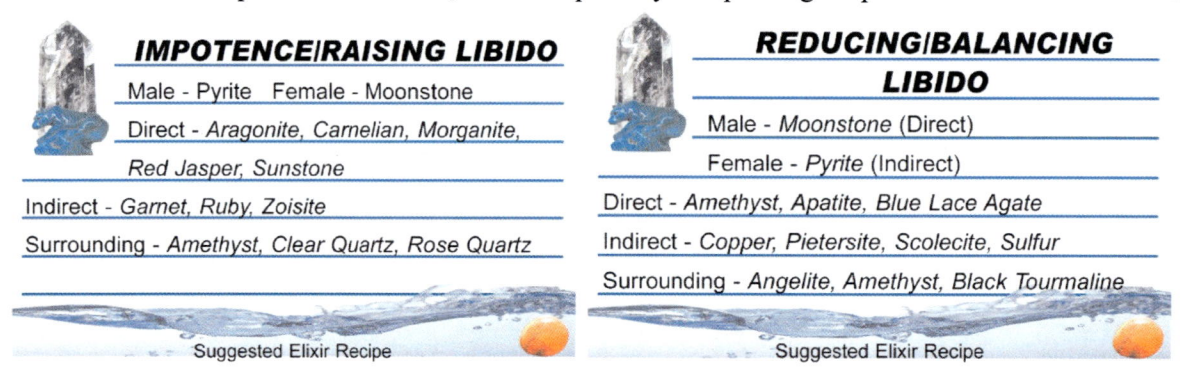

IMPOTENCE/RAISING LIBIDO	REDUCING/BALANCING LIBIDO
Male - Pyrite Female - Moonstone	Male - *Moonstone* (Direct)
Direct - *Aragonite, Carnelian, Morganite, Red Jasper, Sunstone*	Female - *Pyrite* (Indirect)
Indirect - *Garnet, Ruby, Zoisite*	Direct - *Amethyst, Apatite, Blue Lace Agate*
Surrounding - *Amethyst, Clear Quartz, Rose Quartz*	Indirect - *Copper, Pietersite, Scolecite, Sulfur*
	Surrounding - *Angelite, Amethyst, Black Tourmaline*
Suggested Elixir Recipe	Suggested Elixir Recipe

INFERTILITY

Agate – Balances hormones and emotions, strengthens female reproductive organs, enhances fertility, reduces inflammation
Amber – Cleanses, detoxifies, prevents infections, instills vitality, brings out positive emotions and balances hormones
Amethyst – Combat disorders at cellular level, balances hormones, aids metabolism
Auralite 23 – Reduces foreign masses and cells, imparts energy, aids in overall healing,
Azeztulite – Treats cellular disorders and inflammation, detoxifies and regenerates healthy cells and tissues
Azurite – Reduces growths and fibrous masses, cleanses and regenerates good cells, detoxifies body
Bloodstone - Shrinks tumors and growths, revitalizes, treats infections, boosts health of sexual organs

Carnelian – Restores vitality, increases fertility, balances metabolism, aids nutrient absorption, aids female organs
Fluorite – Repairs DNA/RNA cells, reduces growths and small tumors, treats infections
Garnet – Enhances fertility, balances hormones, regenerates DNA, aids with absorption of vitamins and minerals, cleanses blood
Hematite – Reduces scarring and tissue damage, regulates, strengthens and cleanses blood and cells
Jade – Treats infertility, aids in childbirth, beneficial for hips, spleen, detoxifies body, colon and ovaries
Malachite - Treats growths and tumors, enhances reproductive organ health, realigns DNA, boosts fertility
Moonstone – Beneficial for reproductive system, enhances conception and fertility
Morganite – Boosts vitality and fertility while instilling security, balances emotions
Pyrite – Instills vitality and sexual drive, aids male reproductive system, instills sense of optimism
Shungite – Reduces growths and tumors, removes bacteria, toxins and heavy metals, boosts immune system
Sulfur - Shrinks fibrous masses, detoxifies immune system, draws out infections, boosts vitality
Tiger Eye – Heals reproductive system, removes blockages, brings balance to emotions
Zincite - Combats infertility, regulates hormones, beneficial for sexual reproductive system

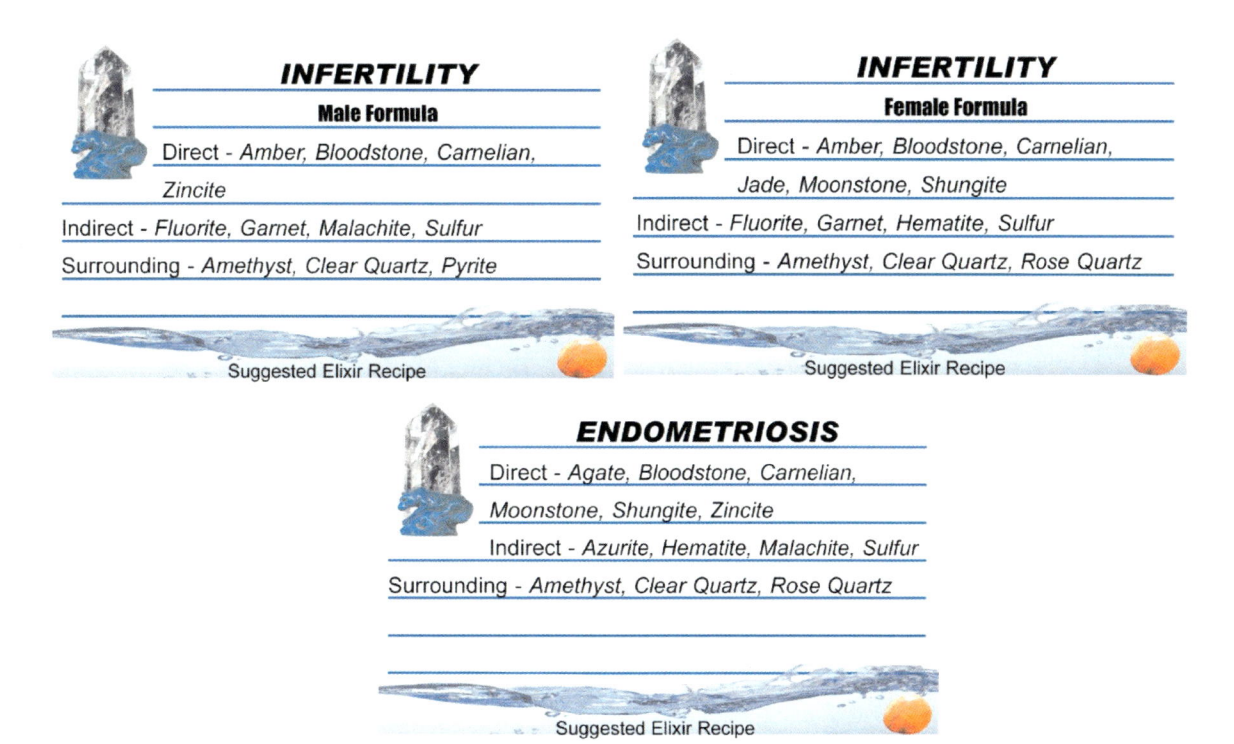

INFERTILITY
Male Formula

Direct - *Amber, Bloodstone, Carnelian, Zincite*

Indirect - *Fluorite, Garnet, Malachite, Sulfur*

Surrounding - *Amethyst, Clear Quartz, Pyrite*

Suggested Elixir Recipe

INFERTILITY
Female Formula

Direct - *Amber, Bloodstone, Carnelian, Jade, Moonstone, Shungite*

Indirect - *Fluorite, Garnet, Hematite, Sulfur*

Surrounding - *Amethyst, Clear Quartz, Rose Quartz*

Suggested Elixir Recipe

ENDOMETRIOSIS

Direct - *Agate, Bloodstone, Carnelian, Moonstone, Shungite, Zincite*

Indirect - *Azurite, Hematite, Malachite, Sulfur*

Surrounding - *Amethyst, Clear Quartz, Rose Quartz*

Suggested Elixir Recipe

INSOMNIA/DREAMS & NIGHTMARES

(Also see Chapter 2 – Gridding)

Amethyst – Calms overactive mind, reduces stress, combats nightmares, enhances dream recall, aids breathing

Apache Tear – Stops nightmares, comforts grief, allows for peaceful, healing sleep

Black Tourmaline – Protection, grounding, reduces negative thoughts and emotions, removes fear

Bloodstone – Calming and reassuring, safety (like in a womb), calms overactive mind and negative thoughts, inspires good dreams

Blue Fluorite – Combats nightmares, calms emotions, energy and erratic thoughts

Calcite- Reduces the effects of insomnia, calms mind and emotions, enhances out-of-body experiences while retains information

Pink Calcite (Mangano) prevents nightmares

Chalcedony – Ends bad dreams, reduces negativity, harmonizes body, mind and emotions

Charoite – Fights insomnia, heal emotions, stimulates spiritual insights and awakenings, aids soul purpose and past life recall

Chiastolite – Past life recall, out-of-body journeying, soul recovery, life purpose, healing, balances emotions

Chrysoprase – Prevents bad dreams, releases negativity, guilt and self-doubt, sense of peace and safety

Hematite – Grounding and tethering stone for out-of-body experiences, balances mind, body and soul, aids in dream recall

Herkimer Diamond – Past life recall and healing, soul purpose, release of negativity, protection, calms mind and stress

Kyanite – Dream recall, reduces fear, strengthens connection to spiritual realm, calms stress

Lepidolite – Prevents insomnia, calms emotions and thoughts, aids with spiritual journeys, releases negativity

Moonstone – Peaceful night sleep, calming and soothing, instills feeling of safety, relieves insomnia and sleepwalking

Prehnite – Protection, peace, alleviates nightmares and fear, aids in healing cause of nightmares

Rhodochrosite – Enhances lucid dreaming, reveals past life, emotional or physical trauma and abuse for healing

Rhodonite – Calms emotions, heals past life, emotional and physical abuse, promotes self love and forgiveness for peaceful sleep

Selenite – Removes negativity, protects, calms and brings peaceful slumber, quiets overactive mind and thought patterns

Seraphinite – Angelic contact, instills sense of security and peace, protection during out-of-body journeys, healing sleep

Scolecite – Reduces stress, calms emotions, reduces negativity and chaotic energy, helps the body to shut down overactive mind

Sugilite – Body, mind and spiritual harmony, soul purpose, past life awareness and healing, promotes emotional calmness and safety, reducing negativity and calming over-stimulated mind

Sulfur – Reduces environmental negativity, overactive thoughts and imagination, brings re-energizing and

healing sleep

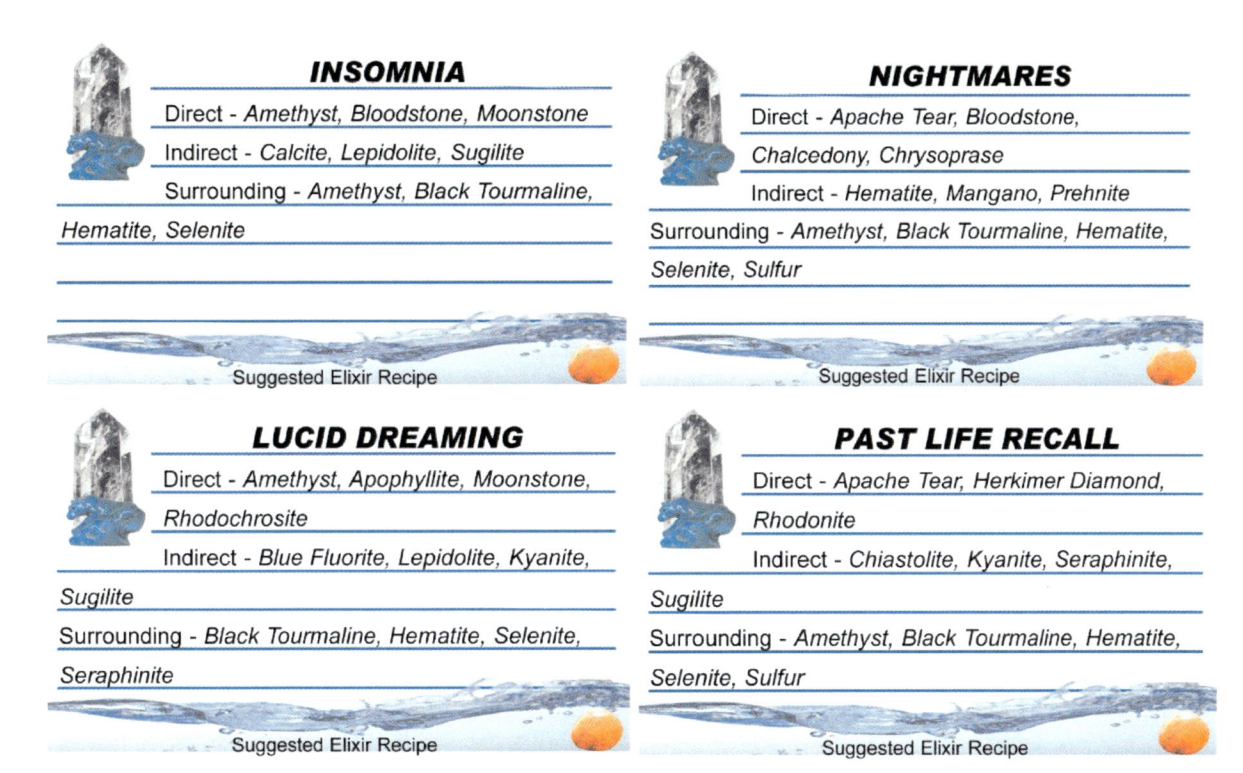

INSOMNIA
Direct - *Amethyst, Bloodstone, Moonstone*
Indirect - *Calcite, Lepidolite, Sugilite*
Surrounding - *Amethyst, Black Tourmaline, Hematite, Selenite*

Suggested Elixir Recipe

NIGHTMARES
Direct - *Apache Tear, Bloodstone, Chalcedony, Chrysoprase*
Indirect - *Hematite, Mangano, Prehnite*
Surrounding - *Amethyst, Black Tourmaline, Hematite, Selenite, Sulfur*

Suggested Elixir Recipe

LUCID DREAMING
Direct - *Amethyst, Apophyllite, Moonstone, Rhodochrosite*
Indirect - *Blue Fluorite, Lepidolite, Kyanite, Sugilite*
Surrounding - *Black Tourmaline, Hematite, Selenite, Seraphinite*

Suggested Elixir Recipe

PAST LIFE RECALL
Direct - *Apache Tear, Herkimer Diamond, Rhodonite*
Indirect - *Chiastolite, Kyanite, Seraphinite, Sugilite*
Surrounding - *Amethyst, Black Tourmaline, Hematite, Selenite, Sulfur*

Suggested Elixir Recipe

KIDNEYS
Agate – Cleanses, balances, and strengthens elimination and endocrine systems, beneficial to kidneys
Amethyst – Removes parasites, cleans, strengthens and detoxifies body fluids and elimination system
Angelite – Balances body fluids, releases toxins and excess water, calms swelling and treats infections
Aquamarine – Strengthens organs, flushes body of toxins and excess fluids
Bloodstone – Detoxifies kidneys and elimination organs as well as strengthens them, heals infections
Calcite – Benefits kidney function and elimination system
Carnelian – Balances and detoxifies body fluids, strengthens kidneys and intestinal tract, beneficial for blood and absorption of vitamins and minerals
Chrysocolla – Treats kidney disorders, strengthens and cleanses circulatory and urinary systems, alleviates pain
Citrine – Combats infections and fever, detoxifies, rejuvenates
Jade – Aids kidneys and adrenals, detoxifies, balances and cleanses bodily fluid
Kyanite – Beneficial to adrenals, kidneys, treats infections and removes blockages
Magnesite – Reduces kidney stone pain, aids in absorption of vitamins and minerals
Peridot – Cleanses, detoxifies, benefits health of kidneys and elimination system, boosts metabolism and energy, aids in dialysis
Rhyolite (Obicular Jasper) – Aids in dissolving kidney stones, nutrient absorption, infections, detoxifies
Ruby – Treats infections, revitalizes adrenals, stimulates and detoxifies kidneys, strengthens organs
Sulfur – Revitalizes, strengthens immune system, reduces swelling and pain

KIDNEYS
Direct - *Agate, Bloodstone, Carnelian, Jade*
Indirect - *Aquamarine, Orange Calcite, Peridot, Sulfur*
Surrounding - *Amethyst, Clear Quartz, Rose Quartz, Selenite, Tourmaline*
Suggested Elixir Recipe

KIDNEY STONES
Direct - *Agate, Bloodstone, Carnelian, Jade, Rhyolite*
Indirect - *Clear Calcite, Chrysocolla, Kyanite, Magnesite*
Surrounding - *Amethyst, Clear Quartz, Rose Quartz, Sulfur, Tourmaline*
Suggested Elixir Recipe

MENOPAUSE/MENSTRUAL ISSUES/MENSOREA

See General Health, Impotence/Libido, Infertility and individual symptoms

Agate (Fire/Blue Lace) – Cools fever and hot flashes, reduces heat while instilling vitality
Amethyst – Balances hormones, metabolism and bodily fluids, reduces pain, eases headaches
Bloodstone - Shrinks fibrous growths, revitalizes, treats infections, boosts health of sexual organs
Carnelian – Reduces excess water, restores vitality, balances metabolism, aids with absorption of nutrients, aids female organs
Charoite – Relieves cramps and pain, cleanses and strengthens circulatory system
Chrysanthemum Stone - Detoxifies, dissolves growths, aids in rebuilding health and immune system
Chrysocolla – PMS, cramping, cycle problems, balances and cleanses blood, treats infections, boosts thyroid and metabolism
Citrine – Cools hot flashes, combats menstrual pain, aid in regulating period
Jet – Eases menstrual cramps, fights infections, reduces bloating
Labradorite – Aids in menstrual cycle, balances hormones, reduces cramps, pain and stress
Lepidolite – Menopause and menstrual cycle, insomnia, re-energizes, dulls pain
Magnesite – Relieves pain, reduces clotting, eliminates cramps, cools hot flashes
Malachite – Menstrual cramps, heals and strengthens female organs, reduces scar tissue, fibrous growths
Moonstone – Regulates cycle, balances hormones, combats water retention, PMS symptoms, cramps
Sulfur – Shrinks fibrous masses and cysts, detoxifies immune system, draws out infections, boosts vitality

PMS/MENSTRUAL CRAMPS
Direct - *Agate, Bloodstone, Carnelian, Citrine*
Indirect - *Jet, Labradorite, Magnesite, Malachite, Moonstone*
Surrounding - *Amethyst, Rose Quartz, Selenite, Sulfur*
Suggested Elixir Recipe

UTERINE SCARRING ASHERTON'S
Direct - *Bloodstone, Carnelian*
Indirect - *Citrine, Jet, Malachite, Moonstone*
Surrounding - *Amethyst, Chrysanthemum Stone, Rose Quartz, Selenite, Sulfur*
Suggested Elixir Recipe

MENOPAUSE

Direct - *Agate, Amethyst, Carnelian, Clear Quartz, Citrine*

Indirect - *Labradorite, Lepidolite, Magnesite, Moonstone*

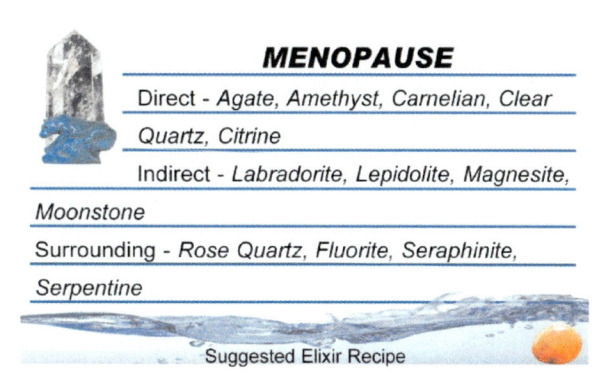

Surrounding - *Rose Quartz, Fluorite, Seraphinite, Serpentine*

Suggested Elixir Recipe

MOUTHWASH - This recipe is also good for tired or sore throats.

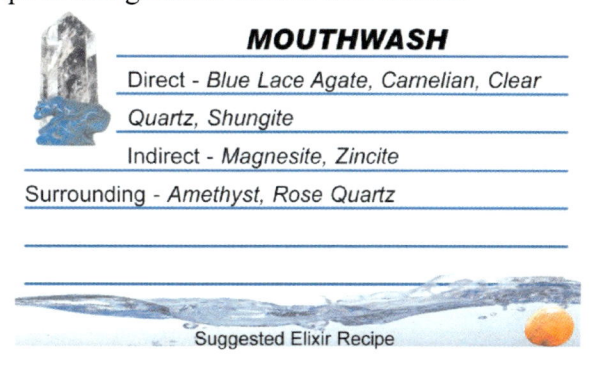

MOUTHWASH

Direct - *Blue Lace Agate, Carnelian, Clear Quartz, Shungite*

Indirect - *Magnesite, Zincite*

Surrounding - *Amethyst, Rose Quartz*

Suggested Elixir Recipe

PLANT BUG SPRAY - This is a natural deterrent for bugs as well as helping your plants to grow.

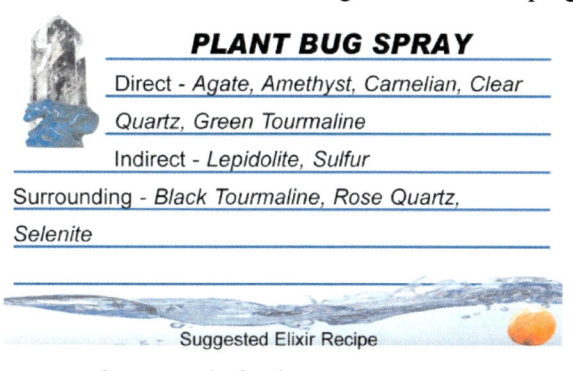

PLANT BUG SPRAY

Direct - *Agate, Amethyst, Carnelian, Clear Quartz, Green Tourmaline*

Indirect - *Lepidolite, Sulfur*

Surrounding - *Black Tourmaline, Rose Quartz, Selenite*

Suggested Elixir Recipe

PROTECTION - Use as a spray perfume or air freshener.

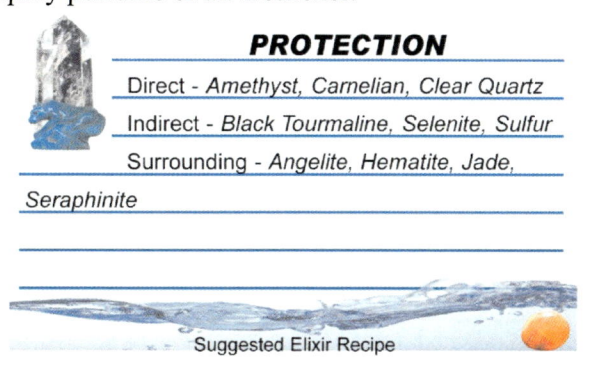

PROTECTION

Direct - *Amethyst, Carnelian, Clear Quartz*

Indirect - *Black Tourmaline, Selenite, Sulfur*

Surrounding - *Angelite, Hematite, Jade, Seraphinite*

Suggested Elixir Recipe

STORMS/WEATHER RELATED CONDITIONS
(See individual symptoms such as headaches, sinuses, muscle pain, etc.)

STORMS/WEATHER

(See individual symptoms such as headaches, sinuses, muscle pain, etc.)

Direct - *Amethyst, Aquamarine. Blue Chalcedony*

Indirect - *Fluorite, Infinite, Sodalite, Super 7*

Surrounding - *Black Tourmaline, Clear Quartz, Gold Obsidian, Selenite*

Suggested Elixir Recipe

SPRING WATER
Use boiled tap water, let it cool a bit then ad these gemstones for a purified spring water taste. You don't need expensive bottled water. I have a half gallon clear glass pitcher which contains these gemstones that I pour my unused boiled tea water into every day. No need to clean the stones.

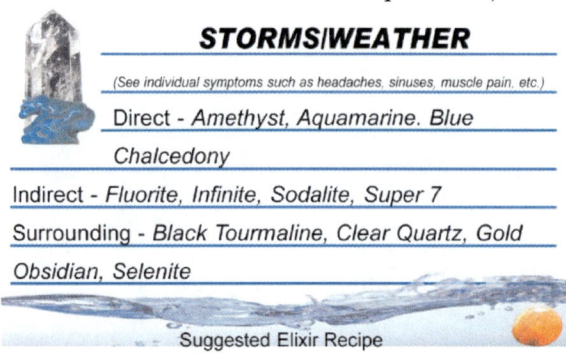

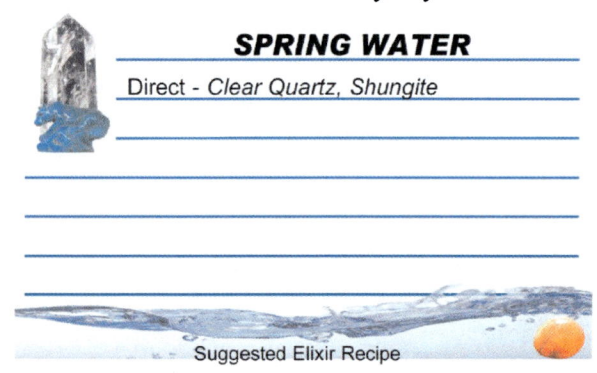

SPRING WATER

Direct - *Clear Quartz, Shungite*

Suggested Elixir Recipe

STUDYING/MENTAL FOCUS/CREATIVITY
Stress is not just for adults; children feel it, too! Peer pressure can create a host of emotional, mental and physical issues that will affect their study and absorption of knowledge. Learning disabilities can make school pure torture for some children. There are quite a few gemstones that will help in different situations and you will need to see which gemstones resonate best with your body or spirit, for each of us reacts differently to each stone's vibration.

Let's start with stress - one of the leading contributors to health issues and learning blockages. There are a variety of stones for stress: Snowflake Obsidian, Kunzite, Sugilite, Serpentine and Fluorite are the top vote-getters to calm the nerves. Each has other metaphysical properties that will also work in the student's behavior.

A really good studying and motivational stone is **Mangano Calcite** for it instills a quest for knowledge, brings focus, memory retention, reduces emotional stress while supporting a feeling of self-worth and self-acceptance. Proper nutrition and growth is one other characteristic of this gentle stone.

For the student that is highly challenged and dealing with a lot of negative peer pressure, **Gypsum** (also known as alabaster or fibrous Selenite) with build strength of character through right action and thought. It molds and shapes lovingly while encouraging growth, quests for knowledge and improvement of intellect.

These stones can be carried in pockets, in book bags, placed next to them on the study table, pieces of jewelry that are worn or can be made into an elixir by using the indirect method of infusion.

Want to create a better study or meditation environment? Place **Sulfur and Salt Crystals Lamps** in the area to increase mental alertness and concentration, reduce stress, and create a positive work atmosphere. They also help to create a healthy environment, and placing chunks of **Rose Quartz and Amethyst** around the room would be helpful as well

Sulfur removes negative thinking, destructive tendencies, willfulness, and distractions of thoughts and emotions. It promotes reasoning skills and decision making. It is energizing, inspiring and stimulates the intellect, while encouraging perfection of self.

Halite or Salt Crystal Lamps elevate a person's mood, while cleansing the air and reducing the negativity. It promotes independence, self-confidence, intelligence, respect, enhances insight and aids in decision making. Rose Quartz instills self-worth, self-acceptance, unconditional love, respect and calms the body, mind and spirit.

Agate – Boosts self-esteem and confidence, calms nerves, increases curiosity and drive, encourages teamwork
Amazonite – Creativity and self-expression, boosts memory retention and thirst for knowledge
Amber – Instills patience, enhances decision-making, boosts memory and clarity of thought
Amethyst – Sharpens focus and meditation, reduces stress, energy, overall health
Apatite – Focus, creativity, communication, self-expression, combats frustration, isolation and separation
Apophyllite – Clear communication, calms fears, reduces anxiety, aids focus and decision making
Aragonite – Sharpens focus and concentration, instills confidence for overcoming obstacles
Azurite – Enhances understanding and memory retention, removes blockages and fears, promotes larger viewpoint
Carnelian – Aids concentration, focus and memory retention, improves decision making and organizational skills
Charoite – Reverses exhaustion, reduces stress and frustration, aids in perception, observation and decision making
Chiastolite – Aids with problem solving and mental abilities, calms fears, aids with transition
Citrine – Calms stress, aids in focusing the mind in learning and understanding information, aids in decision making
Fluorite – Reduces stress, combats shyness, aids coordination and balance, self-confidence, concentration, organization, quick thinking and decision making, memory retention
Emerald – Strengthens memory and decision making, clarity of thought and action, creative expression
Hematite – Aids problem-solving and challenges, focus, concentration and stimulates willingness to learn
Howlite – Memory retention, increases attention to detail and appetite for learning, reduces stress for clear communication
Kunzite – Sharpens focus, aids meditation, allows for self-acceptance, overcomes obstacles, challenges and test stress
Opal – Strengthens memory, stimulates creativity and self expression, stimulates positive attributes and

decision-making

Peridot – Aids focus and mental acuity, re-energizes, learn from mistakes and move forward, instills confidence

Rhodochrosite – Calms nerves and stress, maintain balance and control, self-worth and confidence, retaining knowledge, views all sides of a challenge for resolution

Rhodonite – Inspires one to achieve highest potential, supports confidence, unconditional love, harmony and cooperation

Serpentine - Aids meditation, self-knowledge, self-awareness, and growth. It helps to bring focus and clarity of thought, enhance the intellect, and balance emotions

Snowflake Obsidian – Calms, lowers stress, soothes, aids in focusing the mind to make more receptive to learning and retaining information, promotes intellectual growth, aids in decision making and gaining knowledge from mistakes

Sugilite - Combats fatigue, learning difficulties, dyslexia, autism, promotes harmony with oneself and peers, cooperation, self-confidence, positive thoughts and actions, calms the nerves while eliminating headaches, aids in understanding what is being taught, facilitates memory retention.

Sunstone – Instills confidence, self-worth and leadership qualities, stimulates enthusiasm for overcoming challenges, combats procrastination and negativity

Tiger Eye – Aids in balancing work/play, aids confidence, self-worth, creativity and organization, enhance mental function and acuity, memory retention

Turquoise – Calms, relieves panic attacks, aids in meditation, concentration and creativity, instills 'can-do' attitude

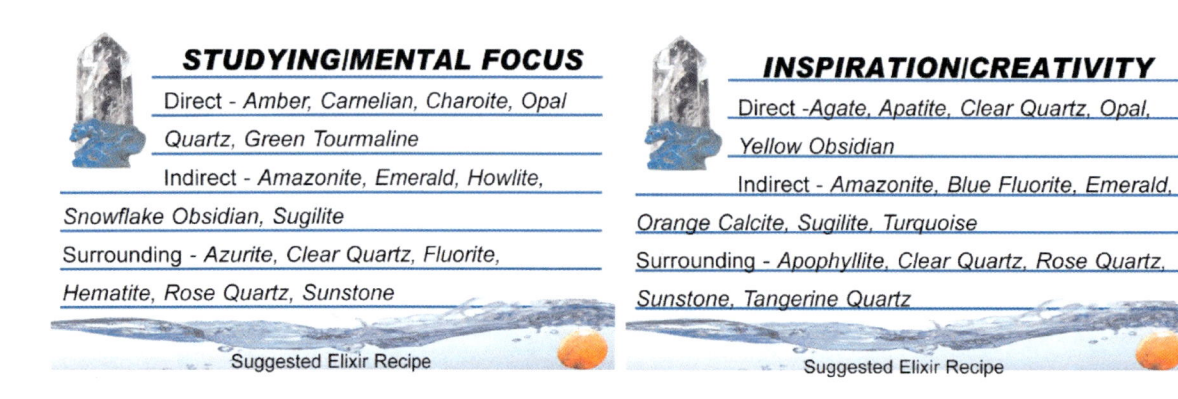

STUDYING/MENTAL FOCUS
Direct - Amber, Carnelian, Charoite, Opal Quartz, Green Tourmaline
Indirect - Amazonite, Emerald, Howlite, Snowflake Obsidian, Sugilite
Surrounding - Azurite, Clear Quartz, Fluorite, Hematite, Rose Quartz, Sunstone
Suggested Elixir Recipe

INSPIRATION/CREATIVITY
Direct - Agate, Apatite, Clear Quartz, Opal, Yellow Obsidian
Indirect - Amazonite, Blue Fluorite, Emerald, Orange Calcite, Sugilite, Turquoise
Surrounding - Apophyllite, Clear Quartz, Rose Quartz, Sunstone, Tangerine Quartz
Suggested Elixir Recipe

THYROID/THYMUS

Amber – Aids thyroid health and treats goiters, stimulates proper function of thyroid, fights infections

Angelite/Blue Celestite – Balances thyroid, reduces inflammation and induces proper function

Apatite – Balances thyroid by stimulating under-activity and reducing over-activity

Aquamarine – Treats thyroid issues to regulate hormones, metabolism and growth, relieves swollen glands

Aventurine – Stimulates thymus and beneficial to adrenals, aids glands and thyroid health

Azurite – Aids thyroid, detoxifies, brings balance and treats under-activity

Blue Lace Agate – Stimulates thyroid and treats infection

Chlorite/Seraphinite – Detoxifies, balances thyroid, aids in nutrient absorption
Chrysocolla – Boosts thyroid and metabolism, balances and cleanses blood, treats infections, boosts thyroid and metabolism
Chrysoprase – Heals goiters, balances hormones and thyroid activity
Citrine – Stimulates thymus and induces proper function of thyroid
Dioptase – Activates thymus, combats fatigue and stress, aids thyroid health
Garnet – Stimulates thyroid and thymus, treats infections, stimulates metabolism, aids nutrient absorption
Jet – Treats goiters and balances thyroid, reduces swelling and pain
Kyanite – Benefits thyroid, thymus, glands, increases metabolism and activity of thyroid
Lapis Lazuli – Combats pain, stimulates thyroid and thymus, boosts immune system
Magnesite – Beneficial for under-active thyroid, boosts metabolism and nutrient absorption, detoxification
Malachite – Reduces growths, balances thyroid function, benefits thymus and glands, detoxifies, boosts immune system
Peridot – Aids thyroid and thymus health, stimulates adrenals, increases energy
Prehnite – Treats goiters, aids thyroid health, stimulates proper function of thyroid and thymus
Sapphire – Calms over-active thyroid and stressed adrenals

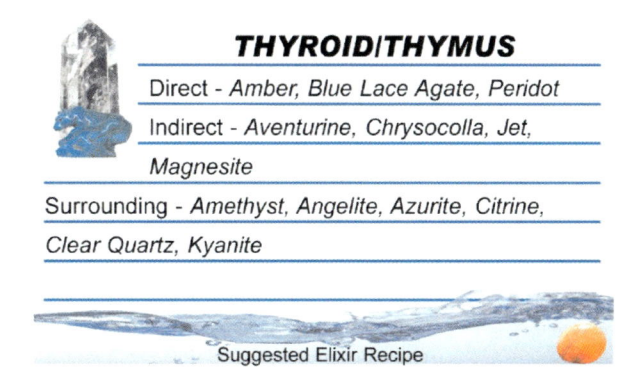

THYROID/THYMUS

Direct - *Amber, Blue Lace Agate, Peridot*
Indirect - *Aventurine, Chrysocolla, Jet, Magnesite*
Surrounding - *Amethyst, Angelite, Azurite, Citrine, Clear Quartz, Kyanite*

Suggested Elixir Recipe

89

INDEX

Aids/Herpes/Infectious Diseases	57-58	Energizing Foot Bath	76
Alcohol/Drug Addition	36-38	Epilepsy/Seizures	66-67
Altars	22	Eyes/Ears/Skin	69-70
Alzheimer's/Dementia/Memory	58-59	Fibromyalgia	54
Angels	34	Financial Stress	28-29
Anger/Grief/Emotional Turmoil	41-42	Food Addiction/Weight Issues	38-40
Antibiotic/Antiseptic	72	Gallbladder/Gallstones/Liver	76-77
Anxiety/Fear	41	General Healt	43
Arthritis	54	Grief	42
Asherton's	82	Hair	77
Asthma/Lung/Respiratory	47-48	Headache/Migraines/Pain Relief	49-50
Autism	73	Healthy Bones/Osteoporosi	52
Back Ailments/Skeletal System	50-51	Hearing	70
Balancing Chakras	17, 20	Heart Disease	55-57
Balancing Cholesterol	57	Herniated/Impacted Discs	51
Blood Disease/Heart Conditions	55-56	High Cholesterol	57
Bone Cancer	61	Immune Building/Colds/Flu/Respiratory	43-45
Bone Spur Removal	52	Impotence/Libido	77-78
Breast Cancer	61	Infertility	78=79
Broken Bones	51	Insect Sting/Fire Ant Bite	72
Cancer/Leukemia/Growths/		Insomina/Dreams/Nightmares	80
Tumors/Fibrous Masses	59-61	Job Stres	27-28
Chemotherapy Side Effects	62	Joint/Nerve/Muscle Pain	52-53
Chronic Fatigue Syndrome (CFS)	62-63	Kidneys	81-82
Cold/Flu/Fevers	45-46	Leukemia	61
Colon/Ovarian Cancer	61	Liver	77
Creativity	86	Lucid Dreaming	81
Crohn's Disease/Colitis/IBS	63-64	Lung Cancer	61
Deodorant	74	Lupus	54
Depression/Mental Anxiety/Fears	41	Lymphoma	61
Diabetes	64-66	Medicine Wheel	23
Direct/Indirect Cleaning	12-13	Memory/Dementia	59
Earth Healing	74-75	Meniere's Disease	70
Edema	75	Menopause/Menstruall Issues/Mensorea	82
Emotional Behaviors/Addictions/Bad Habits	35	Mineral Booster/Rejuvenator	44
Endometriosis	79	Miscellaneous	73

Mouthwash	83	Sciatica	51
Muscle Pain	54	Skin Cancer	62
Nightmares	81	Skin Disorders/Allergies/Sunburn	71-72
Pain/Joints/Bones	49	Sore Throat/Infection Disorders	46-49
Parkinson's Disease/Tremors/Nerve Damage	67	Spiritual Disconnection	32-33
Past Life Recall	81	Spring Water	84
Plant Bug Spray	83	Storm/Weather	84
PMS/Menstrual Cramps	82	Studying/Mental Focus/Creativity	84-86
Protection	8	Surgery Side Effects	62
Quit Smoking/Tobacco	36	Thyroid/Thymus	86-87
Radiation Side Effects	62	Tinnitus	71
Relationships/Relationship Stress	30-32	Viral Infection	46
Respiratory/Bronchitis/Asthma	48	Working with Angels/Guides/Guardians	34
Reynaud's	68		

Made in the USA
Monee, IL
13 September 2024